Praise for *Total C*

"Christmas is meant to be cherished and celebrated, not barely survived due to stress. *Total Christmas Makeover* will help you focus on Jesus, directing your heart to the loving Savior who came to earth. With many practical applications, your Christmas season will become much more meaningful and rich after reading Spoelstra's book."

—**Arlene Pellicane**, speaker and author of *31 Days to Becoming a Happy Mom*

"Are you tired of just letting Christmas happen at your home—and praying merely to survive? No more! Now you and I can be absolutely intentional about embracing all the fun, faith, family, and friendships of this amazing holy season. Melissa Spoelstra's *Total Christmas Makeover* gently guides us through everything seasonal around music, food, scripture reading, extended family gatherings, serving, and especially how to rest in the midst of it all. Under the sections of Ritual, Relationships, and Rest, we discover great new ideas, solid biblical teaching, practical action plans, and a prayer to make it all work through God's help. Best of all, Melissa shares from her own young family's experiences, and we are drawn to realize that though we might fail in some attempts, embracing the coming Christ Child in a fresh way this year is the best gift ever!"

—**Lucinda Secrest McDowell**, author of *Ordinary Graces* and *Dwelling Places*

"Jesus picked a busy time of year to have a birthday! Although I am saying this in jest, there is nothing funny about how the frantic nature of this season can rob one of joy that Christmas represents. In her latest project, Melissa Spoelstra gives candid and practical tools to help the overcommitted and overwhelmed put the merry back into 'Merry Christmas.'"

—**Amberly Neese**, speaker, author, humorist

"This book is light fun and straight to the point with ideas I could actually do with my family. It's a must-read for anyone who starts to freak out when they even hear the word *holiday*!"

—**Kerri Pomarolli**, author, comedian, Hollywood actress

"How many times I've said, 'This Christmas I want to keep my focus off of presents and onto His presence, off of the craziness and onto the stillness, away from commercialism and nestled in the arms of God.' Melissa Spoelstra has given us the perfect 31-day companion to make this desire a reality."

—**Laurie Polich Short**, author of *When Changing Nothing Changes Everything*

TOTAL
CHRISTMAS
MAKEOVER

31 DEVOTIONS TO CELEBRATE WITH PURPOSE

Melissa Spoelstra

ABINGDON PRESS
NASHVILLE

Library of Congress Cataloging-in-Publication Data

Names: Spoelstra, Melissa, author.
Title: Total Christmas makeover : 31 devotions to celebrate with purpose / Melissa Spoelstra.
Description: Nashville : Abingdon Press, [2017]
Identifiers: LCCN 2017022591 (print) | LCCN 2017035482 (ebook) | ISBN 9781501848711 (e-book) | ISBN 9781501848704 (paperback)
Subjects: LCSH: Christmas—Prayers and devotions.
Classification: LCC BV45 (ebook) | LCC BV45 .S66 2017 (print) | DDC 242/.335—dc23
LC record available at https://urldefense.proofpoint.com/v2/url?u=https-3A__lccn.loc.gov
2017022591&d=DwIFAg&c=
GnokDXYZpxapTjbCjzmOH7Lm2x2J46Ijwz6YxXCKeo&r
=ox0wiE5wyqlD4NWBvXI_LEW57Ah1_xv-dTElReAYRyw&m=5MLbr0DL8nuQbujSKI
flKCX3Q6Wz4JGUN3QBYlcfGY8&s=TEV_p07UKcPHmrCCtjoHQkP3QqDrsmnJRgi
W_D_MQO8&e=

17 18 19 20 21 22 23 24 25—10 9 8 7 6 5 4 3 2 1
MANUFACTURED IN THE UNITED STATES OF AMERICA

Contents

Rest

Introduction

Well, December is here, and my kids are already pointing out that we missed the first day of candy in the Advent calendar that hasn't been filled. (I'm pretty impressed that it is already on the wall!)

I have to admit that with each passing year I get less motivated to shop, bake, and decorate; and it has been years since I even considered sending out a Christmas card. I used to brainstorm creative ways to write our family's annual letter with top-ten lists, crossword puzzles, and anything I could dream up to set my letter apart from everyone else's.

As I sit wondering what has happened to my waning Christmas spirit, I also notice that I feel less stressed. Don't get me wrong, I haven't become a total Scrooge. I've done some online shopping and am excited as I envision my children's delight as they open their gifts. I also love looking at the lights on my Christmas tree in the evenings. I don't want to give up on all the Christmas fun; I just want to be more intentional about remembering what this season is all about.

In the past, I often got so caught up in the activity of Christmas that I had no time to spend with the God we celebrate. What a way to say "Happy Birthday, Jesus" by having no time for Him. I want to be sure that I'm not in such a hurry preparing for parties, baking, wrapping presents, decorating, sending cards, and worrying over all these things that I forget to invite Jesus to His own party. So much of it has to do with my attitude and posture toward the things I am doing. I need to slow down and ask:

Why am I doing this?

How will it honor Christ?

How will this activity impact my family?

As I look at Scripture, I see that God initiated and instituted times of celebration. He loves a good party! God gave instructions for the Passover so His people wouldn't forget their deliverance from Egypt. Many times of holy celebration were commanded, such as the festivals of harvest, trumpets, shelters, and the Day of Atonement. These were times of remembrance to help focus on God's character and historical moments of His faithfulness. In looking at these biblical celebrations, I notice three elements included in the festivities:

- **Ritual:** Special activities out of the ordinary routine were planned to help remember what God has done.
- **Relationships:** People spent time together preparing special foods, eating, gathering in holy assembly, and explaining their traditions to children.
- **Rest:** Regular work was to be set aside for planned times of celebration and rest from activity in order to reflect on God.

As I am thinking about my Christmas celebrations, I know many times I have gotten so caught up in the activity of the season that I've lost the meaning behind our traditions. I can't say that most of my holidays have included rest or a lot of time for people in the midst of an overflowing to-do list.

How about you? Do you find that you too have been caught up in the *have to*'s instead of the God-centered *love to*'s?

These thirty-one reflections in *Total Christmas Makeover* focus on prioritizing the rituals, relationships, and rest that will draw us nearer to Christ as we celebrate His birth. Each reading contains thought-provoking questions to ponder, as well as some practical ideas to help us reimagine our holiday.

We can make small changes during this blessed season that can yield big dividends in our pursuit of knowing our Savior who came to earth. God longs for us to draw near to Him. Let's be sure He is invited to own His own birthday celebration this month. Spend the next thirty-one days focusing on the One who came for you. Spend the next thirty-one days with Jesus.

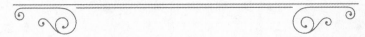

RITUAL

Day 1

REMEMBERING

This is a day to remember. Each year, from generation to generation, you must celebrate it as a special festival to the LORD. This is a law for all time. For seven days the bread you eat must be made without yeast. On the first day of the festival, remove every trace of yeast from your homes. Anyone who eats bread made with yeast during the seven days of the festival will be cut off from the community of Israel. On the first day of the festival and again on the seventh day, all the people must observe an official day for holy assembly. No work of any kind may be done on these days except in the preparation of food.
~ Exodus 12:14-16

When my husband and I got married, we found that our Christmas rituals had some similarities but also quite a few distinctions. My family get-togethers included lots of people overtaking a home and the chaotic opening of gifts, all occurring at once in the room. We had different types of food each year, such as shrimp, pizza, turkey, or ham as main dishes. With so many people gathering, we ate all over the house. Sometimes the routine changed from year to year with different foods, paper plates, and varied formats. One year we might read the Christmas story as a family, and other times we would attend a church service together. I can't recall it always looking the same.

At my husband's family gatherings, Christmas included a perfectly set table, dim lights, and a more formal meal with traditional dishes served. Chaos would not have described anything that went on in his family home during celebrations. Things were orderly, and people were sentimental about the customs being observed each year.

When it comes to our own family Christmas rituals, the most important thing isn't the mode of expression as much as the heart behind it all. Whether your family celebrates formally with firm traditions or more chaotically with varied ways to remember Christ's birth, the key is to remember the why in our observances. Why do we decorate, shop, bake, throw parties, and gather as families during the holidays? We do so to remember Christ.

Our Savior left eternity in heaven and stepped into time. He put on flesh and came humbly to earth as a baby. He came to restore the relationship with God that sin had marred. Jesus came to teach us about our Father—His love, His grace, His holiness, and then to pay the ultimate price to bridge the gap sin created between us. All of this was for us, and this is why we celebrate. When the rituals lose their original intent of helping us remember Christ, we need to rediscover their meaning.

Perhaps some holiday rituals need to be revived or pursued more wholeheartedly, while others should be held loosely and possibly replaced with new ideas. Since many of our Christmas traditions are fun and don't need to be hyper-spiritual, we don't want the commercialized hoopla to cause us to miss the true message of Christmas.

A Christmas makeover doesn't mean throwing out all our traditions and habits over the holiday season and exchanging them for new ones. However, it might mean

- prioritizing the traditions that point us to Christ's birth,
- rediscovering the intent behind the practices we treasure, or
- incorporating some new rituals that will help us share God's message of love with those around us.

Rituals have always been one of the key markers of biblical celebration. When the Israelites left Egypt, God instructed them to hold an annual remembrance and honor the traditions of sacrifice, rest, and preparing special foods that held meaning for them. They were to eat bread without yeast to recall the time when they had to leave in such a hurry there was no time for the bread to rise. The Israelites ate bitter herbs to remember their time of slavery and roasted lamb to commemorate the night the death angel passed over their homes because the blood of an animal was over their doorpost.

God ordained special holy days from generation to generation so His people would not forget His mighty acts. Most Gentile Christians don't celebrate Passover because Christ came as a fulfillment to the foreshadowing of Passover. Jesus shed His own blood as a covering for our sin so that we would not be separated from God. The Gospel of John records, "The next day John saw Jesus coming toward him and said, 'Look! The Lamb of God who takes away the sin of the world!'" (John 1:29).

Jesus is our Passover Lamb. At Christmas, we celebrate His birth while at Easter we remember His death and resurrection. Our holiday rituals are a time to reflect upon Him. Jesus was born to die so that we could have a restored relationship with God. Our Christmas traditions play a part in our remembrance of Him in the midst of our busy schedules, demanding jobs, health challenges, and relational conflicts. We change our routine to include decorations, special events, additional church gatherings, preparing special foods, gift selections, and perhaps a family devotion or special reading. All of this is not to make us stressed out or overwhelmed but to help us remember Christ. So we must carefully contemplate which activities help us focus on God and which stress us out for no good reason.

Every tradition doesn't have to be inherently spiritual, but we must not forget the Savior whose birth we celebrate because we are so busy with candy and cookies. My husband and I found a new normal with our own family. We include both casual and formal elements in our celebrations and other rituals that change over time. When our children were small we read a family devotion that included special ornaments for each day in December. As our kids became teenagers who might not be home every night, we switched to taking turns with teenager-led Christmas devotions that included a craft or creative activity once a week. Sometimes our rituals stay tried and true, and other times they change with age and culture. Any practice can become rote or lose its original intent, so we must evaluate often to be sure our focus is on Christ to make sure He doesn't become forgotten in the midst of Christmas mayhem.

Lord, help me to keep my focus on You this Christmas season. I don't want to forget the importance of Your birth. Help me to remember You often as I prepare to celebrate Your coming to earth. Help me to discern which traditions I should incorporate this year that will draw my attention continually on You and teach me to let go of anything distracting me from the true meaning of Christmas. Thank You for being my Passover Lamb and taking away my sin through Your blood. In Jesus' name I pray, amen.

QUESTIONS FOR REFLECTION

What Christmas traditions did you experience growing up?

Of those activities, which helped you focus most on Christ?

Which of your current Christmas rituals leave you uninspired or stressed out?

What new practices might you incorporate to strengthen your relationship with Christ as you celebrate His birth?

A PRACTICAL APPROACH

One way many families are reminded that Christmas is about Jesus is to have a birthday cake. Since children can relate to their own birthday parties, having a time to sing to Jesus and eat cake helps them remember that Christmas truly is His party! While they receive presents at Christmas, it is the birth of Christ we are truly celebrating.

Day 2

FOOD FOR THOUGHT

The instructions of the LORD are perfect,
reviving the soul.
The decrees of the LORD are trustworthy,
making wise the simple.
The commandments of the LORD are right,
bringing joy to the heart.
The commands of the LORD are clear,
giving insight for living.
Reverence for the LORD is pure,
lasting forever.
The laws of the LORD are true;
each one is fair.
They are more desirable than gold,
even the finest gold.
They are sweeter than honey,
even honey dripping from the comb.
They are a warning to your servant,
a great reward for those who obey them.
~ Psalm 19:7-11

The first time we decided to gather our little family for some Christmas readings from Scripture it was an epic fail. Our son was six years old and loved every minute of it. Our three-month-old mercifully slept during the encounter, but with two-year-old twins, you can only imagine the efforts to enforce listening and discussion. Their attention span resembled that of a gnat at times.

This particular activity was titled the Jesse Tree, which included lessons for December 1st through December 25th. A friend from church shared this activity with me. I thought it might be good for our littles because it included the page numbers from a beginners' Bible we owned that had pictures and simple stories. The guide provided instructions to gather or make ornaments to wrap each day. We made the ornaments ourselves with construction paper or Shrinky Dinks since we couldn't find a fiery furnace or Ten Commandments ornament in any store!

Creation is the first lesson within the Jesse Tree activity, which includes stories such as Noah, Abraham, Jacob, and others following up to Christ's birth. On the first night, my husband read the Creation story from the children's Bible and showed the pictures in the book. We opened the ornament that contained a globe and put it on the tree. All was going fairly well until we came to the review questions. My husband started with one he thought would be fairly easy.

"Who made the world?"

One of the twins exclaimed, "I did it! I made the world!"

Our daughter looked to us to compliment her, but my husband said, "No, come on. Who made the world?"

This time, much less confidently, she stated in a questioning tone, "Mommy did it?"

If comprehension of truth and remembering what God had done was our goal, we had certainly missed the mark. Although we laugh about this story now, we did continue in our pursuit of using this activity year after year by reviewing Bible stories and incorporating Scripture readings into our Christmas ritual. While we have switched gears because of our frenetic schedules of teenagers and a college student, we still want to pursue taking time to gather and read Scripture together.

As you reflect on the coming holiday season, how can you

incorporate a ritual of Scripture reading? Whether you gather as a family with children or teenagers, or just spend some quiet moments each day reading alone or with your spouse, having a plan with God's Word is the kind of ritual that helps us reconnect with the message of Christmas. When we aim for nothing, we hit it every time.

The Jesse Tree is only one of many options. You will find many more ideas by asking your friends, searching on the internet, creating your own plan, or checking out some of the ideas that I have collected from others at the end of today's reading. Reading God's Word helps us realign our thinking with God's truth. As our thought life centers on His character, His love, and the sacrifice of sending Jesus to earth, it affects our attitude. Humility, gratefulness, and contentment are all attitudes that are impacted by our thinking patterns over long periods of time.

Of course, we need God's Spirit to transform our thinking. One of the ways He does this is through the Scripture. Just as we eat a physical diet, our spirit is fed by what enters our bodies through our eyes and ears. If all we consume is mindless television shows or movies, social media feeds of everyone else's lives, or music and books with worldviews that contradict Christian values, we can become spiritually malnourished. Not all soul junk food is inherently evil; it just doesn't bring health and life to the human spirit. God's Word has cleansing power to help us remember God's love and truth. Daily consumption is highly recommended as a ritual during the holiday season to guide us in remembering His heart in sending His one and only Son into the world.

Whether you get your family involved in gathering for some special reading each day, week, or even just on Christmas morning, be intentional in including the Bible as part of your Christmas ritual this year! Don't beat yourself up if you miss a time or don't finish everything you set out to do. Instead, celebrate the progress you make and the closeness with Jesus you experience as you allow God's Word to be alive and active in your life.

Lord, give me a hunger and thirst for Your Word. Guide me in knowing how to implement a Christmas ritual of reading Scripture. Give me discernment whether I am to do this on my own or include other family members or friends. Direct me to plan and help me to be disciplined in seeing it through. Show me where any soul junk food is causing me to be spiritually weak. Strengthen me by Your powerful and holy Word. In Jesus' name I pray, amen.

QUESTIONS FOR REFLECTION

What plans for reading Scripture have you used in the past during the holiday season?

Consider what barriers keep you from reading God's Word daily on your own or with others during the holidays.

Is there a simple plan God is calling you to put into action to make reading God's Word a priority in your family's routine?

A PRACTICAL APPROACH

There are so many great reading plans you can use to incorporate reading Scripture into your Christmas rituals. If you are just looking for a plan to do on your own, check out the YouVersion app on your phone or device with a daily reading plan for December.

If you are looking for a ritual to use with your family, it is good to consider age levels and attention spans. While sometimes you may want to stick with a cherished family tradition, trying something new might reignite the energy to get into God's Word. Many reading plans and devotional books are available for either daily or weekly times. Here is one idea for each that I have personally used and recommend:

Daily: The Jesse Tree has twenty-five daily readings including instructions for making ornaments for each day. It starts with Creation and hits many key stories that lead up to the birth of Christ.

Weekly: Purchase an Advent wreath that includes Scripture readings. Light a candle for each week representing hope, peace, joy, and love. Then light the Christ candle in the center on Christmas Day.

Somewhere in-between: Write Scripture references on craft paper and wrap different pieces of a Nativity set. Put one under the tree each night for your children to open each morning so they can read a part of the Christmas story each day.

Day 3

PRAYER

I pray that from his glorious, unlimited resources he will empower you with inner strength through his Spirit. Then Christ will make his home in your hearts as you trust in him. Your roots will grow down into God's love and keep you strong. And may you have the power to understand, as all God's people should, how wide, how long, how high, and how deep his love is. May you experience the love of Christ, though it is too great to understand fully. Then you will be made complete with all the fullness of life and power that comes from God.
~ Ephesians 3:16-19

A few weeks ago I found myself with some extra time. I had a few hours before I was scheduled to speak at an event in another city. Because I was in a hotel room, there was no laundry to do, errands to run, or chores to complete. I remember thinking how it would be great to spend some time in prayer. While I had dialogued with the Lord here and there, it had been a while since I had taken a chunk of time to spend dedicated to prayer. I piddled around the room, straightening things from my suitcase, and finally settled in on my knees. I felt distracted and wondered if I should answer emails since I had the benefit of Wi-Fi. After all, I could pray on the plane, but I couldn't work on my laptop. My internal conversation revealed a battle against the discipline of prayer.

Thankfully I talked to myself instead of listening to myself. Even though my flesh didn't want to pray, I knew my spirit desperately needed some focused time in God's presence. I began praising God.

I confessed sin and thanked Him for so many blessings in my life. Then I poured out my heart with personal requests as well as things for my family, friends, and the long list of concerns written in my journal. The closeness I felt with Jesus as I sat quietly and listened was priceless. There is an intimacy with Christ that only intentional prayer can bring.

So why do I fight spending time in prayer? Why don't I want to do it? Why do other things seem to crowd out prayer so often? Every time I actually take the time to pray, I am blessed and so glad I did it. I can never remember regretting time spent with the Lord in prayer.

Is there any chance that you struggle alongside me? I've met many people who share my struggle to be disciplined in prayer. God tells us to pray. Jesus modeled it in His own life and even taught us in the Gospels how to do it. If I must battle how to spend the time when I'm alone with no distractions, the busy flow of the holidays only compounds the opposition to taking time to pray. Because of this, we must fight to make the time and attention to pray during the Christmas season.

Of course, we don't have to be alone or on our knees to pray. We can talk to God while driving in the car, exercising, baking cookies, or really doing anything. However, there is a difference in the intensity of focus when we are multitasking and praying. I'd rather pray while doing other things than not pray at all, but I think we should persevere in finding some time to be still in prayer.

Jesus went out to a remote place to pray. Where is a quiet place where you could meet Jesus alone during the holiday season? In the movie *War Room*, the main character used a closet as a special place to meet with Jesus. Honestly, my living room rug is the location where I most frequently find myself on my knees or on my face with the Lord. As you reflect upon your prayer life, where do you pray most often?

The place isn't as important as the ritual itself, but having a special location to meet with Jesus can serve as a prayer reminder.

This holiday season, consider choosing a new location in your home for prayer. Is there a special chair, a closet, or a window seat that could be a place to celebrate the Savior's birth in prayer? After you've selected a location, next you'll need to set a time. We aren't talking about carving out an hour each day. Maybe start with only five or ten minutes. By making the goal manageable, you'll be more likely to keep the appointment. What if you set your alarm for ten minutes earlier and shared your morning coffee with Jesus? Perhaps you're a night owl, and before you turn in at night, you'll stop at your special location to praise, confess, thank, and ask!

Prayer is one of our most powerful ways to stay close to Jesus, and yet it is often neglected during the very holidays we set aside to remember His birth. As you think about one or two small changes you can make in your prayer life this season, consider these verses in Scripture regarding prayer: "The earnest prayer of a righteous person has great power and produces wonderful results" (James 5:16). "Never stop praying" (1 Thessalonians 5:17).

Lord, I love talking and listening to You in prayer, but sometimes I struggle to be disciplined in it. Help me to make time with You a priority. Teach me to pray. As I celebrate Your birth this month, I long to know You more. Show me where I can meet with You in a special place. Give me the discernment to see which time of day would be best to be still in Your presence. Help me to be dedicated in meeting You there. Lord, I want to know You and be a prayer warrior for others as well! In Jesus' name I pray, amen.

QUESTIONS FOR REFLECTION

Where do you regularly find time to spend focused time in prayer?

What distractions do you battle in the discipline of prayer?

What minutes can you carve out today to spend talking and listening to your Savior?

A Practical Approach

As Christmas cards are mailed to your home, collect them in a basket. Then at mealtimes, pull out one of the cards and pray for the individual or family who sent it. Pray for their health, for their holiday to be meaningful, and for any concerns you might know of from your relationship with them.

Day 4

MAKE A JOYFUL NOISE

The Magnificat: Mary's Song of Praise

Mary responded,
"Oh, how my soul praises the Lord.
 How my spirit rejoices in God my Savior!
For he took notice of his lowly servant girl,
 and from now on all generations will call me blessed.
For the Mighty One is holy,
 and he has done great things for me.
He shows mercy from generation to generation
 to all who fear him.
His mighty arm has done tremendous things!
 He has scattered the proud and haughty ones.
He has brought down princes from their thrones
 and exalted the humble.
He has filled the hungry with good things
 and sent the rich away with empty hands.
He has helped his servant Israel
 and remembered to be merciful.
For he made this promise to our ancestors,
 to Abraham and his children forever."
~ Luke 1:46-55

One time when I was speaking at an event, the coordinator mentioned that at the end, the speakers, comedian, and worship leader would all come up on stage to lead in a final song. I laughed and said, "Will our microphones be turned on?" Apparently I was the only one who could not carry a tune. I asked that the sound man be careful to turn my mic off. I celebrate the gifts God has given me, but unfortunately making a joyful noise by singing is not one of them.

When my kids were little, my husband asked me not to sing to them. He said he wanted them to have a chance. He wasn't being unkind; his family is very musical, and his strong bass voice has some real talent. I've accepted that singing isn't one of my gifts. I have often joked that Jesus is the only one who loves my worship. Even without this talent, I love to sing. Worship is something that helps me get out of bed on Sunday mornings. Celebrating in song is something we were created to do.

I remember sitting at a country concert years ago and watching the crowd passionately raise their hands and sway to the music. I remember thinking, *We were created to worship.* If we don't worship the Lord, we will find something else to admire in song.

One of the rituals of biblical celebration includes singing. Mary, the mother of Jesus, sang a song called the Magnificat right after her cousin Elizabeth blessed her. Her soul magnified the Lord. She made God bigger through her worship. She magnified Him.

Like a microscope or a magnifying glass, we make God bigger in our lives as we sing of His glorious attributes. We tell Him we trust Him, and we thank Him for choosing to use us. Mary sang her heart out. Her life wasn't easy. I wonder how many believed that Mary's pregnancy truly resulted from the Holy Spirit? Commentators estimate that Mary could have been around fourteen or fifteen years old at the time the angel Gabriel visited her. I have a fourteen-year-old daughter. If she came to me and told me she was pregnant, and that God was the father, I am unsure of what my reaction would be.

I wonder what Mary's neighbors thought? What about her parents? Her cousin Elizabeth believed and blessed her, but her calling wasn't easy. Yes, all generations since have called her blessed, but what about her daily life? She accepted God's call and sang in worship to God.

One of the rituals of the Christmas season that helps us draw nearer to God is singing. Whether you have the voice of an angel or something more like my musical abilities, celebratory worship in song should be included in your Christmas traditions. We can sing in the car alone. We can join with others to sing Christmas carols in our neighborhoods, at nursing homes, or gathered as families while we put up decorations. After all, "The best way to spread Christmas cheer is singing loud for all to hear!" according to a Christmas movie character named Buddy the elf. While this source isn't exactly scriptural, it is difficult to sing and be grumpy at the same time.

The words of our traditional Christmas carols are full of theological truth. Some are somber and reflective like "Silent Night." The lyrics were written in 1818 by an Austrian assistant priest, Joseph Mohr. The church organ was broken, so he wrote a song the day before Christmas that could be sung with just the use of a guitar. Other carols, such as "Angels We Have Heard on High," remind us of the heavenly choir. "Away in a Manger" recounts the humility of Christ's birth and His coming to earth. "We Three Kings" speaks of the gifts brought to Jesus from Eastern royalty. "O Little Town of Bethlehem" reminds us of the place across the globe where Mary and Joseph made a home with Jesus.

These songs, and many like them, are rich in reminders. Christmas music helps us remember that this time of year is special. We change our routines, and even our music selections, so that we don't forget something very important. God sent His Son to earth. Mary sang a song with humble acceptance and embraced her calling. The angels sang a song of rejoicing that the Prince of Peace had come. God's goodwill toward us is throughout the pages of Scripture, and Jesus is the pinnacle of that grace toward us.

Even if your voice resembles mine, we still sing. Even if Christmas brings back memories of a difficult childhood or the death of a loved one, we sing. We celebrate what God has done. He loved us enough to send His one and only Son. That is good news worth singing about! Take a few moments right now to sing your favorite Christmas song. If others are in the room, you can sing it silently in your head. If no one else is around, belt it out like the angel chorus! Celebrating in song is a ritual that will draw us back to the reason for the season!

Lord, You give me a reason to sing. I want to worship You with music but also with my life. Help me to take the posture of Mary in humble acceptance of Your calling. Please let the songs of the season touch my heart in a new way. May the familiar words not lose their meaning but help me rediscover the joy of Your birth. Teach me new songs, Lord, that I might continue to worship You with fresh melodies that ignite my heart with passion to exalt You. In Jesus' name I pray, amen.

QUESTIONS FOR REFLECTION

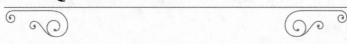

What are your favorite Christmas songs? Why do they touch you so deeply?

How does music change your mood or attitude?

In what Christmas rituals do you participate that include celebrating through music?

A PRACTICAL APPROACH

Consider these ideas for celebrating in worship during the Christmas season:

- Join your church choir or musical group and sing to the Lord as your audience during both rehearsals and performances.
- Gather your small group or ministry team to sing carols at a nursing home or retirement center.
- Ask some families from your neighborhood to carol from house to house with you one night in December.
- During your church Christmas Eve service, pay attention to the songs. Whether it is the children singing or a candlelit "Silent Night," worship God with your heart, mind, and soul as you sing in gratitude for His coming to earth.

THE LIGHT
OF THE WORLD

*"The people who sat in darkness
  have seen a great light.
And for those who lived in the land where death casts its shadow,
  a light has shined."*
~ Matthew 4:16

*Jesus spoke to the people once more and said, "I am the light of the world. If
you follow me, you won't have to walk in darkness, because you will have
the light that leads to life."*
~ John 8:12

*Jesus replied, "My light will shine for you just a little longer. Walk in the
light while you can, so the darkness will not overtake you. Those who walk
in the darkness cannot see where they are going."*
~ John 12:35

*For God, who said, "Let there be light in the darkness," has made this
light shine in our hearts so we could know the glory of God that is seen in
the face of Jesus Christ.*
~ 2 Corinthians 4:6

One of my favorite Christmas rituals comes at the end of most
December days. When all the kids have finally gone to bed and
exhaustion beckons me to do the same, I love to pause in my living
room. I sit on the couch and just take a moment to turn off all the
lights except the glowing softness of string lights wrapped around our
tree and banister. I take in the calm for just a moment and remember

why we decorate with lights. Jesus came to earth. We are the people who were in great darkness. Sin separated us from God, but through the Christ Child, we can be reconciled to God.

The light through God's one and only Son breaks through the darkness of sin. I know that we don't know the actual date of Christ's birth. I know Christmas has become commercialized and lost its original intent at times but rather than debate whether decorating trees was a pagan practice or get hung up on how we should celebrate, let's redeem the traditions we already have in place.

Darkness can be scary. We feel alone, can't see our way, and might even bump into things. Without Christ's light, our lives are dark. We lack purpose, power, and the ability to draw near to a holy God. Because of Christ we can see things more clearly. We have hope in a dark world.

As we put up our tree, we can remind ourselves and our families that Jesus came as a baby but died on a tree. As we string up lights or drive around to look at them, let's focus on Jesus' statement that He is the Light of the world. When we make wreaths, decorate our mantles, or get out special holiday dishes, we can remember that we do things differently for a purpose. We change the look of our surroundings as a ritual to celebrate something great. God loves us. His plan was to redeem us through Christ.

The concept of decorative items for the purpose of remembering important truths is not foreign to Scripture. When the Israelites were wandering in the wilderness, God instructed them to set up the Tabernacle as a reminder of His presence with them. God said He would dwell there and meet with them. In Numbers 8, we find that God instructed the leaders to prepare lamps. God said, "When you set up the seven lamps in the lampstand, place them so their light shines forward in front of the lampstand" (Numbers 8:2). In verse 4, we find that this lampstand was made of beaten gold and designed with decorative blossoms.

The Lord had instructed the people to set up the Tabernacle in the center of the camp with all the tribes camped around it. He wanted the lamps to never go out and shine forward as a constant reminder that they were not alone. He was with them. Even in the dark of night they could catch a glimpse of the lamps burning in the Tabernacle.

God's people no longer meet with Him in a tabernacle. Christ broke through the darkness. He is the Light of the world. He calls us to shine His light forward just as these lamps were to shine their lights forward. Jesus said in Matthew 5:16, "Let your good deeds shine out for all to see, so that everyone will praise your heavenly Father."

As you untangle strands of lights or ignite the wick of a simple candle, remember that your life is meant to shine bright in a dark world. Your decorations are not just another item on your to-do list, they are a ritual with meaning. When you take in the beauty of light this holiday, take some time to thank God for sending Jesus. God doesn't call us to hide his light under a bushel. No! He asks us to shine out our good deeds so that everyone can praise the Father.

Where is the Lord calling you to shine your light?

- Is there a family you can help who is in need of some gifts?
- What encouraging words can you speak to someone who is grieving this Christmas?
- How can you shine your light at your church, work, or family Christmas parties?

We enjoy sitting in the glow of the light, but we are to be a conduit for it. Christ is the light, and we allow Him to shine through us for the glory of God. Second Corinthians 4:7 says, "We now have this light shining in our hearts, but we ourselves are like fragile clay jars containing this great treasure. This makes it clear that our great power is from God, not from ourselves." We can't create the light, but we can shine it through our lives. Whether you put up a few decorations or deck the halls and go all out, don't lose the wonder and the why of every light!

Jesus, You are the Light of the world. Thank You for breaking through my own personal darkness. Sometimes life can still feel dark. Help me to cling to Your light and shine it to those around me. Like the lamp in the Tabernacle, I want to shine my light forward. Help others to see Your light in my attitude, words, actions, and the smile that Your light brings to my face. Ignite my soul to shine brightly for You. In Jesus' name I pray, amen.

QUESTIONS FOR REFLECTION

Where are some places you see lights placed in honor of the Christmas season?

When in your daily routine can you stop and enjoy the beauty of these lights?

Where is God asking you to shine your light forward in your sphere of influence?

A PRACTICAL APPROACH

Consider these ideas when searching for opportunities to celebrate Jesus during the Christmas season:

- Set aside a special night for your family to look at lights. Before you leave, read together John 8:12 or 2 Corinthians 4:6 and talk about why lights are important at Christmas. (They help us remember that Jesus is the Light of the world.)
- When it is time to get out your Christmas decorations or go pick out your Christmas tree, spend a few moments together talking about why you observe this tradition. Remind your family that it is not just about making things look pretty or because you do it every year. Talk about the ritual of changing your surroundings to remember an important spiritual truth. Make any connections you can between your rituals of decoration and the story of Christmas. Here are just a few examples:

  1. Do you have an angel or star on the top of your tree? Explain to your family members the role of the angels and star in the Christmas story.
  2. Read a story about the history of the candy cane and include them in your decorations.
  3. Although some of your decorations might be "just for fun" or tied to your cultural heritage, mention to your family that fun is a big part of celebrations!

Take the time to tell stories and ask questions so the next generation won't miss the meaning behind your holiday decorating rituals.

Day 6

TASTE AND SEE

Taste and see that the Lord is good.
*   Oh, the joys of those who take refuge in him!*
~ Psalm 34:8

When you enter the land the LORD has promised to give you, you will
continue to observe this ceremony. Then your children will ask, "What does
this ceremony mean?" And you will reply, "It is the Passover sacrifice to the
LORD, for he passed over the houses of the Israelites in Egypt. And though
he struck the Egyptians, he spared our families." When Moses had finished
speaking, all the people bowed down to the ground and worshiped.
~ Exodus 12:25-27

One of my favorite holiday parties each year is with my international cooking class. Ladies from all different nationalities meet once a month, rotating homes to prepare a meal together. The hostess plans the menu and gathers the ingredients; we show up with our cutting boards and knives and work together to make some sort of authentic cuisine associated with a certain country. I've learned to make so many interesting meals with ingredients I don't regularly use. I've enjoying joining in with others to make Chinese dumplings, Russian borscht, French cordon bleu, and some things with tofu and seaweed I could never serve to my brood.

The last time I hosted, twelve different nationalities were represented. Our holiday party is the most special. Instead of cooking together, we all bring a traditional holiday dish from our home country. Then we go around the room and share what the holidays were like for us growing up. Not everyone celebrates Christmas, but we learn about Chinese New Year celebrations and other expressions of faith. I love hearing from my South American friends about the huge Nativity displays in yards and waiting until midnight to put the baby Jesus in the manger.

As you reflect on some of the Christmas rituals from your childhood, I wonder if some of them revolve around food? Meals bring people together as we stop school, work, and regular routines to eat with people we love. Sometimes our special foods are related to our heritage or family traditions. My husband is of Dutch descent. He makes a special New Year's treat from batter and apples deep fried and loaded with powdered sugar. My kids look forward to Appelflappen each year. Other times we create new traditions in our celebration.

Biblical celebrations included food. In fact, when rest was mandated for the Passover celebration God instructed them, "On the first day of the festival and again on the seventh day, all the people must observe an official day for holy assembly. No work of any kind may be done on these days except in the preparation of food" (Exodus 12:16).

God instructed the Israelites to eat special foods during the Passover as a reminder of what He had done. They were to eat

- unleavened bread because they left Egypt in such a hurry there wasn't time for the bread to rise (Exodus 12:20),
- a lamb to remember that the death angel passed over their homes because the blood of a lamb was put on their doorposts (Exodus 12:21), and
- bitter salad greens representing their bitter life of slavery in Egypt (Exodus 12:8).

They were to pass these traditions on to future generations so the people would not forget the mighty act of God rescuing His people from Egypt. While we don't have food associated with Christmas celebrations prescribed in the New Testament, we do celebrate God's great rescue. He sent His Son to earth to save us from our sins. Our food rituals can be another chore on our list of things to do, or they can serve as a reminder of the sweetness of our God.

As we roll out cookies with our children and decorate them, we can talk about God's goodness. We might even share with them the verse from Psalm 34:8, "Taste and see that the LORD is good." Whether we bake fudge or seven kinds of cookies or put together a store-bought gingerbread house each year, our food rituals can remind us that

- we are blessed with an abundance of food,
- our God is good, and
- He rescues His people from the slavery of sin.

Christmas is a time when we give gifts to each other to remember that Jesus is the greatest gift. When we gather with family to bake special cookies, cakes, or breads, often our intent is to share them with others. Another biblical celebration comes to mind when I think of this tradition. In the Book of Esther, God again rescued the people of Israel. A man named Haman had tried to kill all the Jews, but God used a woman named Esther to help them. Once more, the people were to celebrate a festival each year called Purim so they wouldn't forget God's mighty salvation. During the festival they were to give gifts of food to each other. "He told them to celebrate these days with feasting and gladness and by giving gifts of food to each other and presents to the poor. This would commemorate a time when the Jews gained relief from their enemies, when their sorrow was turned into gladness and their mourning into joy" (Esther 9:22).

God has turned our mourning into joy through His Son, Jesus.

Christmas provides a great opportunity to give gifts of food to others. If you make more sweet treats than your family really should consume, consider wrapping some to share with others this season.

God, I have tasted and seen that You are good. Lord, I pray the time I spend in the kitchen this holiday season will give me another reason to focus on You. Thank You for the provision of food and sweet treats You have provided for my family. I'm grateful for the way food brings my family and friends together. Help me to keep thoughts of Your rescue at the center of all my Christmas rituals! In Jesus' name I pray, amen.

QUESTIONS FOR REFLECTION

What are some of the foods you especially enjoy during the holiday season?

What memories of your childhood revolved around meals and food?

How can you share the abundance of food God has provided to you as gifts to others?

A PRACTICAL APPROACH

Write Psalm 34:8 on a notecard and place it in your kitchen. As you bake, cook, or wash dishes, praise God for His goodness in your life. Use that time to pray for others who don't enjoy the blessing of pantries and freezers full of food but truly depend on God for daily bread.

Make an extra batch of your favorite treats and wrap them up with a note of thanks and Christmas blessing for your

- mail carrier,
- kids' teachers,
- Sunday school teacher,
- Bible study leader, or
- anyone who blesses your family behind the scenes whom you might overlook.

Day 7

GOOD AND PERFECT GIFTS

When they saw the star, they were filled with joy! They entered the house and saw the child with his mother, Mary, and they bowed down and worshiped him. Then they opened their treasure chests and gave him gifts of gold, frankincense, and myrrh.
~ Matthew 2:10-11

Whatever is good and perfect is a gift coming down to us from God our Father, who created all the lights in the heavens. He never changes or casts a shifting shadow. He chose to give birth to us by giving us his true word. And we, out of all creation, became his prized possession.
~ James 1:17-18

"You parents—if your children ask for a loaf of bread, do you give them a stone instead? Or if they ask for a fish, do you give them a snake? Of course not! So if you sinful people know how to give good gifts to your children, how much more will your heavenly Father give good gifts to those who ask him."
~ Matthew 7:9-11

When I was a girl, the anticipation of gifts was a huge part of our Christmas. On Christmas Eve, we gathered at my grandparents' house with all of our cousins, aunts, and uncles and spent several hours opening gifts. Then we went home and woke up on Christmas morning to our own family gifts. While I wouldn't say we were overly spoiled, I remember the wonder of unwrapping a Strawberry Shortcake lunch box, Cabbage Patch baby, or Barbie doll swimming pool with great excitement.

39

For many children, Christmas means getting presents. So why do we do all this shopping and wrapping and planning? We give gifts at Christmas to remember that Jesus is the greatest gift. We also find that gifts were brought to the baby Jesus. While the wise men look good in our Nativity sets, we learn in Scripture that they were never actually at the stable. They came later when Mary and Joseph were living in Bethlehem. We don't know exactly how many kings visited the Christ Child, but we know they brought three presents along with them.

These weren't just any gifts. They were costly items that were presented to royalty or deity in the ancient world:

- Gold is a precious metal.
- Frankincense is an expensive perfume or incense.
- Myrrh is a valuable anointing oil.

Receiving these items would have changed the financial picture for Mary and Joseph. We don't know what they did with them. They might have kept them and treasured them as reminders of how special this child they were entrusted with really was. It's possible they sold them in order to finance their flight to Egypt when Joseph was warned in a dream to flee Bethlehem. No matter what became of them, we give gifts at Christmas to remember the incredible journey of the men from the East. They traveled far while following a star in order to see the baby sent from God.

We celebrate God's greatest gift to us in sending His Son to earth. He left heaven and came down to earth to teach us about the Father. Then He gave His very life on the cross to save us from our sin.

In a world that has become so commercialized, it is difficult to keep Christ at the forefront of gift giving. We can reclaim the ritual of giving this holiday season. God is the ultimate Giver of gifts. His presents are the absolute best. Take a minute to read about His provision in Matthew 6. Every good and perfect gift comes down from the Father of lights (James 1:17).

God is the greatest giver. Recognize that God is the source of everything good in our lives. Everything we have comes from Him. He has given us

- clean water to drink,
- food to eat,
- shelter,
- clothing to wear,
- all sorts of technology to enjoy,
- the gift of time,
- friends and family with whom to share life,
- abilities and talents to equip us for work,
- work that enables us to provide for others, and
- rest for body, mind, and soul.

I'm sure you could add to this list of gifts. Everything we have finds its source in our loving Creator. Take a moment to thank God for the gifts in your life.

God invites us to ask Him for what we need. Just as we know how to give good gifts to our children, God longs to give us what is best for us. One of my greatest joys of the holidays is watching my children open their gifts. Their faces light up as they receive whatever treasure we have purchased for them. As teenagers now, they usually have a pretty good idea of what is under that tree for the simple reason that they make lists. I ask them to email their wishes to me with links on where to purchase them. I sort through them and decide what to buy. This year one of my girls sent me an image of a glitter pillow that was overpriced and, quite frankly, a little bit ugly. I decided to cross it off mainly because her room is a mess and her bed is rarely made. That pillow would end up under a pile of clothes on the floor and not bring her much joy.

God invites us to ask for what we want. He may sometimes say yes, but other times He may know that the thing we ask for isn't the best choice for us. Other times the answer is "not yet." Like a good parent, He delights to give us good gifts, but He gets to decide what is best.

It is better to give than to receive. Our kids love Christmas Eve after our church service. We come home and they open their gifts to each other and my husband and me. We started this tradition when they were very small. They would save up their allowances in anticipation of our shopping day. We would all go to the dollar store together. My husband would stay in the car with three of the kids while I would take one in to shop. He or she would choose something for each sibling and my husband, and I would turn my head as my gift was selected. We would label the bag and place it in the back of the car. I would then take in the next child and repeat the process. At home I would help them wrap their gifts individually as they admired their choices. On Christmas Eve, each child would delight to see the recipients open the gifts. They would explain with excitement why they chose the gifts they did. Now that they are older, they do their own shopping and spend more than one dollar on each other. Yet they still find the joy that comes from giving!

Gifts are a fun and exciting part of Christmas, and we must prayerfully prioritize the best gifts. Perhaps we might scale back in some areas in order to be generous in others. Gifts of time and talent are often more treasured than monetary or material gifts. As the Holy Spirit leads, give generously and enjoy the ritual that finds it's meaning in the greatest gift of all—Jesus.

Lord, change my attitude when it comes to gifts. Help me to remember that You are greatest giver of gifts. I want to be like You. Give me wisdom in choosing gifts for the people in my life. Help me make good choices that will bring joy to each recipient. Lord, I am asking You for the gift of _____ (peace, hope, joy, reconciliation, and so on) this season. Thank You for giving me just what I need. I want to learn to be satisfied with all that You have provided for me. In Jesus' name I pray, amen.

Questions for Reflection

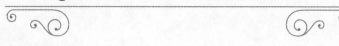

What is your typical attitude toward gift buying during the holidays? Is it a chore or a delight? How can the ritual of gift buying, wrapping, and receiving help you think about Jesus this year?

What gift from God can you thank Him for today?

What gift are you asking God for this Christmas?

A PRACTICAL APPROACH

Several of my friends buy their children three main gifts each Christmas to help them remember that the wise men brought Jesus three gifts. This keeps things simple and Scripture focused. The children may receive other gifts from family members, but the gifts from their parents are just three things.

Day 8

OFFERINGS

Remember this—a farmer who plants only a few seeds will get a small crop. But the one who plants generously will get a generous crop. You must each decide in your heart how much to give. And don't give reluctantly or in response to pressure. "For God loves a person who gives cheerfully." And God will generously provide all you need. Then you will always have everything you need and plenty left over to share with others. As the Scriptures say,

> *"They share freely and give generously to the poor.*
> *Their good deeds will be remembered forever."*

For God is the one who provides seed for the farmer and then bread to eat. In the same way, he will provide and increase your resources and then produce a great harvest of generosity in you.

Yes, you will be enriched in every way so that you can always be generous. And when we take your gifts to those who need them, they will thank God.

~ 2 Corinthians 9:6-11

Once when my youngest child was around six years old, she was looking through a book we used as a prayer guide at mealtimes. It had pictures and information about many different countries with specific prayer requests. Some of the pages gave information about general people groups rather than actual nations. My daughter came to me with the page opened to a chapter called, "Children on the Street." It showed kids sleeping in alleyways in a third world country. With tears in her eyes she asked me if some children really slept in streets. I told her that it was true. She pleaded with me to take her that moment to find these children and bring them to our home.

I was at a loss for words to explain how far away these children lived and how we couldn't just go take them. I remember feeling broken at how callous and forgetful I can become about the plight of poverty across the globe. My daughter's heart was breaking for things that also break God's heart. I pray she never loses that tenderness.

One of the rituals of Christmas is generosity. What some refer to as the Christmas spirit is really God's Spirit. He is generous. When we offer back to God some of what He has provided for us, we get the chance to be like Him. He calls us to give cheerfully and from the heart.

In the Book of Numbers, the Lord gave instructions for regular offerings to be brought that would provide for the priests and Levites (Numbers 18). God instructed the people to bring the best of their animals, grain, and oil to offer to Him. During festivals and holy days, special offerings were to be presented to the Lord (Numbers 28). Generosity is one of the rituals of celebration.

While we should remember those in need throughout the year, Christmastime gives us pause to focus on helping others. At times, I've been tempted not to include my kids in some of the extra opportunities to give that are presented at Christmastime. When our small group provides gifts for local families in need, it is easier to order gifts online. Operation Christmas Child boxes are fun to fill, but waiting until after school when the kids are home isn't always convenient. Yet these extra offerings during the holidays can be a great time to express generosity and also teach it to the next generation.

Our giving should be regular and proportionate to our income (1 Corinthians 16:2). However, we find that special holidays are times for extra offerings. If we get a Christmas bonus at work or receive monetary gifts from others, we can share a portion with those in need. The challenge often comes in choosing where to invest our extra gifts. My mailbox and email inbox are full of requests from great organizations making pleas for support during the month of December. While we can't give to everyone who asks, we can prayerfully ask God's Spirit to direct us in our generosity.

Jesus taught that it is better to give than to receive (Acts 20:35). When we plan well and give sacrificially of our best, we experience the peace and joy He was talking about. A few times the Israelites gave their defective leftovers as offerings, and God wasn't too pleased about it (Jeremiah 24). It's not that God needs our money. He owns the cattle on a thousand hills (Psalm 50:10), but He designed us to be generous. Living His way brings Him glory and us abundant life. He challenges us to give because it is good for us.

Generosity is the one area where God challenges us to test Him. Malachi 3:10 says, " 'Bring all the tithes into the storehouse so there will be enough food in my Temple. If you do,' says the LORD of Heaven's Armies, 'I will open the windows of heaven for you. I will pour out a blessing so great you won't have enough room to take it in! Try it! Put me to the test!' " God longs to bless us. He wants to use us as His hands and feet so that children in our towns and across the globe have their basic needs met. Your offerings can make a huge difference in the lives of others when it comes to clean water, medical care, food, and gifts they couldn't afford without some assistance.

Today, ask the Lord to direct your ritual of giving. Offer Him your life, including your bank account, and watch Him open up the windows of heaven to pour you out a blessing!

Lord, I want to be like You. You are generous to me. Thank You for all You have provided in my life. Guide me with the resources You have entrusted to me. Show me where You would like for me to give special offerings this Christmas. I believe that it is better to give than to receive. Help me to handle Your money wisely so that I can be a generous giver like You! In Jesus' name I pray, amen.

QUESTIONS FOR REFLECTION

How can you express generosity with extra offerings this holiday season?

Is there a need you know of that you can meet anonymously?

What organizations that are doing great work both locally and around the world can you support financially?

A PRACTICAL APPROACH

Consider these ideas for helping others:

- Research local organizations that are making a difference in your community and see how you can best support them. Our town has a great Christian organization that runs an Adopt-a-Family program at Christmas. It's a great time to shop for a family in need with specific requests and sizes. Gather your small group, Bible study members, or ministry team for a fun night of shopping and wrapping as well as praying for a specific family.
- Operation Christmas Child is always in need of shoe boxes filled with items for children in other countries.
- Christmas is a great time to connect with missionaries or orphans you support. Get creative and ask questions to find what would be most beneficial to help others this Christmas!

Day 9

SERVING

*Then James and John, the sons of Zebedee, came over and spoke to him.
"Teacher," they said, "we want you to do us a favor."*

"What is your request?" he asked.

*They replied, "When you sit on your glorious throne, we want to sit in
places of honor next to you, one on your right and the other on your left."*

*But Jesus said to them, "You don't know what you are asking! Are you
able to drink from the bitter cup of suffering I am about to drink? Are you
able to be baptized with the baptism of suffering I must be baptized with?"*

"Oh yes," they replied, "we are able!"

*Then Jesus told them, "You will indeed drink from my bitter cup and
be baptized with my baptism of suffering. But I have no right to say who
will sit on my right or my left. God has prepared those places for the ones he
has chosen."*

*When the ten other disciples heard what James and John had asked,
they were indignant. So Jesus called them together and said, "You know
that the rulers in this world lord it over their people, and officials flaunt
their authority over those under them. But among you it will be different.
Whoever wants to be a leader among you must be your servant, and whoever
wants to be first among you must be the slave of everyone else. For even the
Son of Man came not to be served but to serve others and to give his life as a
ransom for many."*

~ Mark 10:35-45

One of the members at my church leads a large campus ministry
at one of the nation's biggest universities. He said that he often
receives emails from people offering to "refresh" his students by
speaking or playing music at their weekly meeting. He appreciates
the offers but also finds it puzzling that no one has ever asked to

serve in a way that the campus leaders believe would be to the best benefit to the students. People have a variety of spiritual gifts and talents and often look for opportunities to use those gifts to benefit others, but sometimes God calls us to just serve. Serving may not be glamorous or accompanied by fame or even appreciation. During Christmas, serving sometimes includes scissors, tape, and wrapping paper. Other times it involves flour, sugar, and a rolling pin. These are some of the items we use often during the Christmas season. Why do we practice these rituals? We serve those we love by wrapping up thoughtful gifts and baking sweet treats. Jesus said that He came to serve rather than to be served.

Many of our Christmas rituals involve serving our families, but we can also help our families engage in the joy of serving others. Our world often sends messages through commercials or media that we deserve to be served. Yet Jesus calls us to a reverse economy. He said that we should be different. Our goal should be to serve others rather than vie for position or prestige. James and John wanted assurances that they would be able to sit in places of honor. Jesus reminded them that places of honor are often accompanied by suffering.

Our aim should be to serve others. Many opportunities to do that often pop up during the holidays. In our church body, we have two young women who have each just given birth to their first child. With trepidation, I sent out the email asking for people to sign up to bring meals. I know people find themselves stretched with family, parties, and extra responsibilities, but I am praying that God will raise up others to serve in this very tangible way.

This is also a time of year when people are generous with their resources. Volunteers are needed to facilitate the season of giving by

- ringing bells to collect funds;
- sorting food and gifts;
- counting money;
- delivering meals or gifts to families in need;
- cooking, cleaning, or serving meals at a shelter;
- stocking goods or taking inventory; or
- manning drop-off stations.

One of my friends spent a morning greeting people who live in the streets, asking about their needs and seeking to meet as many as possible. Others will quietly serve behind the scenes in the nursery during candlelight services on Christmas Eve. God gives us so many opportunities to be His hands and feet. We can't do it all, but we can ask the Lord to give us eyes to see the needs in front of us.

Serving others requires sacrifice. It costs something to love others extravagantly. It might mean staying up later, even though we are tired, or saying no to an activity we enjoy in order to help someone else. I have to admit that there have been times when I have dreaded serving. I work with the middle school students at my church. I love them to pieces. Yet, just recently I was brainstorming excuses to skip the midweek Christmas party.

I was tired. My to-do list was overflowing. I bargained with God that the night was more social than spiritually focused with lots of food and a white elephant gift exchange. I knew I needed to go. Once I got there and made connections with students, I felt energized. Often I don't look forward to serving but then feel so blessed on the drive home. Serving can be like that.

Can you relate to feeling the nudge to serve but fighting the excuses in your head? Let God's voice win out. Serve sacrificially this week and experience the joy of being different. Don't worry if anyone else saw or heard that you did a good deed. Do it just for God's glory and bask in the joy that serving brings.

God, You are the ultimate Servant. You came and showed us what it means to truly serve. Show me when, where, and how You are calling me to serve others this season. Help me to use the gifts and opportunities You give me for Your glory. I confess that sometimes I can be like James and John who wanted positions of honor. Help me to let go of titles and embrace humble service. In Jesus' name I pray, amen.

QUESTIONS FOR REFLECTION

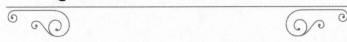

What are some practical ways you serve your family on a regular basis?

What needs and opportunities to volunteer are currently available?

How is God calling you to serve that will require a sacrifice of your own personal time or comfort? How can you live out that calling?

A PRACTICAL APPROACH

Involve your family, Bible study, or small group in a least one practical way to serve this season:

- Volunteer to ring the Salvation Army bells for a few hours. One family I know came with their musical instruments and sang and played music to bless those around them as they rang the bells.
- Partner with your church or a local organization that provides food or gifts for families in need. Don't tell them how you want to serve; ask them what would be the most helpful for them!
- Many people travel during the holidays so children's ministry directors often struggle to cover nursery and classes. Offer to help even before the need is presented.
- Ask local teachers how you can help them serve the children in their classrooms. One year we provided shoe boxes with small gifts and practical items for every student in an inner city school just to bless the families in the community.

Day 10

SOMETHING OLD AND SOMETHING NEW

One day some people said to Jesus, "John the Baptist's disciples fast and pray regularly, and so do the disciples of the Pharisees. Why are your disciples always eating and drinking?"

Jesus responded, "Do wedding guests fast while celebrating with the groom? Of course not. But someday the groom will be taken away from them, and then they will fast."

Then Jesus gave them this illustration: "No one tears a piece of cloth from a new garment and uses it to patch an old garment. For then the new garment would be ruined, and the new patch wouldn't even match the old garment.

"And no one puts new wine into old wineskins. For the new wine would burst the wineskins, spilling the wine and ruining the skins. New wine must be stored in new wineskins. But no one who drinks the old wine seems to want the new wine. 'The old is just fine,' they say."
~ Luke 5:33-39

One of my children's highlights on Christmas morning is searching for their hidden stockings. My husband composes a poem with the parameters of the search and places it on the kitchen table to be found on Christmas morning. As soon as they wake they read the poem to find clues as to whether they should look outside or not and what areas are off limits. It also lists the earliest time that parents are allowed to be woken up. I don't know any other families whose children scour the house or backyard for stockings. Last year my college-age son found his on the roof of our home! (Clearly mom was not consulted on the hiding of the stockings that year!)

This isn't a spiritual ritual, and it isn't a tradition passed down from either of our parents. It is just something my fun-loving husband decided to do when the children were small. It became a favorite, so we kept it going each year. Other Christmas rituals we practice because they were passed down for generations. A candlelight Christmas Eve service, having Christmas family devotions, baking cookies, and exchanging gifts are a few of the traditions we experienced as children and want to re-create with our own family. As we think about our Christmas rituals, the important thing is to consider what God is leading us to do from year to year. We can ask questions such as:

- Will this activity draw us nearer to Christ and thoughts about His birth?
- Will it bless others?
- Will it deepen our relationships with family and friends?
- Will it bring laughter and fun?
- Will it offend anyone who is grieving or hurting during this season?

We must also remember that some rituals are right for some and not others. Some people questioned Jesus as to why the disciples of John the Baptist and the Pharisees were fasting, yet His followers were feasting and drinking. This helps us remember the truth of Ecclesiastes 3:1, "For everything there is a season, a time for every activity under heaven." For some, the holidays are a time of grief as they remember loved ones who have passed or have a broken relationship and need space to be alone. For others, Christmas is a season full of happy memories and celebration. Christmas rituals are not one size fits all.

As we consider what practices to incorporate from year to year, we must draw near to God and realize change is one of the only constants in our lives. What worked for us as kids might not be right for our children or grandchildren. We must be careful not to put new wine into old wineskins. This means exercising flexibility and considering others when it comes to our Christmas rituals.

Are there some traditions you go along with because your extended family wants you to? Even if looking at lights, wearing Christmas pajamas, or following someone else's schedule isn't your favorite, we must learn to think of others and seek wisdom from God about when to do things we don't enjoy to honor the rituals of others. Sometimes we break from old practices to institute new ones. Even if we celebrated Christmas Eve a certain way for years, it is okay to start something new. For many years we went over to a friend's home where a large group of people gathered after our church Christmas service. Our children loved all the food and playing with friends. However, as our children got older, they preferred to go home and exchange gifts. We began watching *The Nativity*, a movie that tells the story of Christ's birth together every Christmas Eve. We transitioned from one ritual to another.

We can do this because there is a time for every activity under heaven. Jesus said His disciples feasted while He was with them, but they would fast later. Christmas rituals aren't set in stone. They morph and change as the years go by. The important thing is to keep Christ at the center of all we do so that our eyes stay fixed on Him.

Lord, help me to hold tightly to the traditions that draw me near to You. Show me where to loosen up and be prepared for change when it comes to new rituals. Help me not to dig my heels in and always have to have it my way. I want to put You first in my life and think of others second. If there is an area where I am trying to force new wine into old wineskins, please show me where I am off course. I want to live Your way and embrace fresh ideas for learning ancient truths. In Jesus' name I pray, amen.

QUESTIONS FOR REFLECTION

What are some Christmas traditions that you inherited from extended family?

What are new traditions that you have instituted in your immediate family and friendships?

How do you handle conversations about plans with family or friends where you don't like the conclusions?

When others participate in rituals you wouldn't choose for yourself, how do you respond?

A Practical Approach

Consider the following when establishing rituals for your family:

- Make a list of all the rituals you participate in during December. Put a star next to all the ones that you initiated. Put a circle next to those you would rather not participate in but feel obligated. Evaluate whether your list is balanced or not.

- When planning holiday gatherings, work together with friends, in-laws, and extended family members with a humble attitude and remember that there is a time for everything—even doing things you don't want to do.

- Brainstorm a list of your ideal Christmas rituals. If you could celebrate any way you wanted, what would it look like? Then consider how those changes would affect others. Ask the Lord what fresh ideas He might lead you to incorporate into your holiday season.

RELATIONSHIPS

Day 11

SCENERY AND MACHINERY

"So now I am giving you a new commandment: Love each other. Just as I have loved you, you should love each other. Your love for one another will prove to the world that you are my disciples."
~ John 13:34-35

Love each other with genuine affection, and take delight in honoring each other.
~ Romans 12:10

Love is patient and kind. Love is not jealous or boastful or proud or rude. It does not demand its own way. It is not irritable, and it keeps no record of being wronged. It does not rejoice about injustice but rejoices whenever the truth wins out. Love never gives up, never loses faith, is always hopeful, and endures through every circumstance.
~ 1 Corinthians 13:4-7

I was lost in thought as I pulled up to pick up my daughter from work. She got in the front seat as I was still working something out in my mind. I don't even remember what it was. Maybe I was thinking about what I would make for dinner or what other errands I needed to run while I was out of the house. Finally, I heard a persistent, "Mom, Mom?" break into my reverie. "Are you okay?" my daughter asked. I told her I was fine, that I was just thinking about something. She said I had completely ignored her as she began to tell me about her shift. I apologized. I hadn't meant to be so self-absorbed.

I find it easy to take this posture during the holidays. As I think about all I need to do, I lose sight of the value of the people around me. If I'm not careful, people can become scenery and machinery—the mail carrier who brings my packages ordered online, the waitress bringing my food, or even my own daughter sitting in the front seat of the car with me. They are real people with real stories. They have reasons for joy and also difficult circumstances.

As I read about the early biblical celebrations of Passover, Tabernacles, Purim or the harvest celebrations, I notice that people are central. Slowing down to celebrate meant gathering with others to eat, rest, and connect. While the holidays bring many gatherings, we must fight to be fully present. Even when we are surrounded by people, we can become preoccupied, distracted, or isolated in our own worlds.

The Scriptures we read today speak of love. We are called to love one another. Over and over the Bible speaks to how we should "one another." We should:

> "Love one another." (John 13:34 NIV)
> "Outdo one another in showing honor."
>   (Romans 12:10 ESV)
> "No longer criticize one another."
>   (Romans 14:13 HCSB)
> "Serve one another through love."
>   (Galatians 5:13 HCSB)
> "Carry one another's burdens."
>   (Galatians 6:2 HCSB)
> "Accepting one another in love."
>   (Ephesians 4:2 HCSB)
> "Always pursue what is good for one an-
>   other." (1 Thessalonians 5:15 HCSB)

There are many additional "one another" commands found throughout the Bible. We can't "one another" alone. Our next ten days of devotions will focus on relationships. Christ came for people—not projects, events, décor, or stuff. Only two things will truly last forever: the souls of people and the Word of God. Connecting with people should be a priority during the holiday season. Sometimes we do this side-by-side making cookies in the kitchen or serving at our church Christmas brunch. Other times we sit face-to-face talking with a friend at a party.

I need to be reminded of this often because my introverted tendencies often pull me inward. Scripture tells us that our love for one another will prove to the world that we follow Jesus. We can't do this on our own. We need God's help to love His way. Someone once told me that she wanted to be a "there you are" kind of person rather than a "here I am" type. How about you? What would others say about you? Do you ask your coworkers, family members, servers, or even the check-out person at the grocery store what is going on in his or her life? Is your posture curiosity and concern for others, or are you preoccupied with your life and circumstances? When I walk into a Christmas party, event, or family gathering, I often pray and ask God to make me a "there you are" kind of person. I don't want people to fade into scenery and machinery. I want to value them. As I read the Gospels, I find Christ to be a very much "there you are" type. He spoke to children, answered questions patiently, and never seemed to be in a hurry. As we celebrate His coming, let's follow His example in loving people.

Lord, help me to see others as You see them. Help me to love them with Your unconditional love. I don't want to get so caught up in my world that I lose sight of others. Help me to look people in the eyes, to ask good questions, and to discern when people are hurting. I want to be Your hands and feet to love those You have put in my path. Show me how to do it and give me the courage and strength to put relationships over tasks. In Jesus' name I pray, amen.

Questions for Reflection

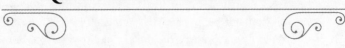

Can you relate to being lost in the reverie of demands?

What people who you may be overlooking are right under your nose?

How is God calling you to love others today?

How can you make people a priority this Christmas?

A PRACTICAL APPROACH

Write a note of thanks with a small gift card or home baked good to those who serve you on a regular basis. Here are some people to consider:

- mail carrier
- bank teller
- barista at a coffee shop you visit often
- server at a restaurant you go to regularly
- clerk at a store you frequent
- child's music teacher or sports coach
- receptionist at your doctor's office
- exercise instructor or trainer
- Sunday school teacher
- Bible study leader
- doctor or nurse

This could be anyone with whom you cross paths regularly. Ask God's Spirit to bring people to mind and help you see those around you as He does. To be appreciated and noticed by others encourages those who work hard year-round to enrich our lives.

Day 12

GOING ALL OUT

That night there were shepherds staying in the fields nearby, guarding their flocks of sheep. Suddenly, an angel of the Lord appeared among them, and the radiance of the Lord's glory surrounded them. They were terrified, but the angel reassured them. "Don't be afraid!" he said. "I bring you good news that will bring great joy to all people. The Savior—yes, the Messiah, the Lord—has been born today in Bethlehem, the city of David! And you will recognize him by this sign: You will find a baby wrapped snugly in strips of cloth, lying in a manger."

Suddenly, the angel was joined by a vast host of others—the armies of heaven—praising God and saying,

"Glory to God in highest heaven,
and peace on earth to those with whom God is pleased."
~ Luke 2:8-14

My friend Elizabeth was the kind of person who went all out for people. At baby showers she didn't buy off the registry. She made special blankets by hand for each new mom. You could often hear her laugh across the room after church services as she talked about her kids or her Lord. She filled a room with her smile and a contagious energy.

Last Christmas Elizabeth unexpectedly passed away. One day she was her exuberant self, and the next she was gone. Her entrance into heaven has caused me to think a lot about going all out. We serve a God who goes all out for us. I love how He announced the birth of the Messiah. Our Father definitely made a big show with a host of angels on a hillside declaring the good news that He was sending a Savior.

One of the cool things to me is that the Lord went all out for shepherds. They were poor, dirty, and often outcasts of society. These are the ones God went all out for! The lowly shepherds got to hear the news of the Messiah's birth in an incredible way long before religious leaders or those the world values as important.

As I reflect on God's extravagant love, I wonder how we can follow His example and go all out for others? Elizabeth did it with homemade blankets and encouraging words. This meant taking extra time and energy to make others feel special. In order to go all out for people in our lives, we'll need God's Spirit to guide us in the who, how, and when. We can't go all out for everyone. In order to love my husband extravagantly, I might need to scale back time with my friends. To go all out for a person in need, I may have to sacrifice in other areas.

My mentor, Deb, has loved me extravagantly for almost twenty years. She is generous with her time and wisdom, and she loves to spoil my family. Going all out doesn't necessarily mean spending more money. It's not the American motto of bigger, better, faster, and more. Instead, going all out means sharing God's love with others in a way that is meaningful to them.

I feel loved by Deb because she knows me. She knows my favorite drinks. She can tell when I'm tired or discouraged. Loving people extravagantly starts with knowing them. When we really are familiar with someone, we can go all out in ways that are meaningful in their situations. God knew what we needed when He sent His Son. We were lost in sin and desperate for redemption. Our sin separated us from an intimate relationship with our Creator. Jesus came to earth to remove the penalty of sin through His blood. God went all out so that our relationship with Him could be restored.

I want to go all out for others, but I often have a tendency to overlook them. My personality tends to be more task-oriented while my husband is more people-oriented. Christmas can be one of those times when we all skim the surface of trying to do so many things at once. Instead, we need to focus on God and seek His help to discern where to spend our time and resources to love extravagantly.

When I think about my friend Elizabeth, I realize that life is fleeting. We don't know how much time we will have to go all out for people. I reflect back and hope that she knew how loved and appreciated she was. Tomorrow isn't promised, so we need to go the extra mile in loving people today!

As you think of those whom God has placed in your sphere of influence, who might He be calling you to go all out for? Is there someone in your life who needs to know they are

- known,
- valued, and
- extravagantly loved?

Once you have identified the who, then comes the how. What gift of time, creativity, words, or some material good might cause them to experience a touch from God through you?

Take a few moments now in God's presence to seek His wisdom on how to "go all out" for one person this week!

Lord, thank You for your extravagant love. Thank You for sending Your Son to earth so that I can know You. Help me to go all out for others! Show me who I can encourage in a special way. Give me Your mind to know who needs a reminder of Your great love, and guide me in going all out in extravagant love. In Jesus' name I pray, amen.

QUESTIONS FOR REFLECTION

Who can you "go all out" for this week?

What will you need to let go to make the time and space to go all out?

What are some specific ways others have loved you extravagantly?

How can you see God loving you extravagantly in the midst of difficulties lately?

A Practical Approach

Here are some ideas to consider to go all out for others:

- Meet a financial need anonymously. Someone in our church had my pastor-husband send out an email asking everyone in the church to think of any coworkers, neighbors, or friends who might need financial help to make Christmas special. My husband then delivered the gifts anonymously to strangers who had no idea where the gifts came from.
- Forgive that person who hurt you! Forgiveness is a great way to go all out with God's love.
- Take the time to write a note to someone at work, church, or a family member telling them specifically what you appreciate about him or her.

Day 13

PROPOSING

"God blesses those who are humble,
for they will inherit the whole earth."
~ *Matthew 5:5*

"Take my yoke upon you. Let me teach you, because I am humble and gentle
at heart, and you will find rest for your souls."
~ *Matthew 11:29*

"So anyone who becomes as humble as this little child is the greatest in the
Kingdom of Heaven."
~ *Matthew 18:4*

"Tell the people of Jerusalem,
'Look, your King is coming to you.
He is humble,
riding on a donkey—riding on a donkey's colt.' "
~ *Matthew 21:5*

"But those who exalt themselves will be humbled, and those who humble
themselves will be exalted."
~ *Matthew 23:12*

Getting along is so hard. One of the things that makes it difficult is our tendency to project our thoughts, feelings, and beliefs onto others. Our default is to think:

- What annoys me also annoys everyone else.
- What doesn't bother me shouldn't bother anyone else.
- If I need time to process things, so does everyone else.

- If I don't need time to process, then you shouldn't either.
- When I know the right way, I should keep pushing until everyone acknowledges that my way is right.

You get the idea. When Jesus came to earth, He came humbly. His first bed was a manger. I can imagine Mary cleaning out any food debris or animal slobber before laying the King of the universe inside. Later, Jesus rode humbly on a donkey and instructed His followers to seek the humility of children. He called us to be teachable and not think we already know everything.

If our cup of life is already full, and we think we know all that we need to know, there is no room for a different viewpoint, a lesson learned, or a new insight. In order to be truly humble and teachable, we must leave room in our cup to learn.

Yet often I want to dig in my heels just like the self-righteous Pharisees, clinging to my own way. How can we step outside our own way of feeling and thinking and see other's points of view? In the midst of trying to understand those around us, how do we stay true to how God has wired us and hold fast to our beliefs?

One thing that has struck me lately is an observation someone made at a conference I attended. The speaker said, "Jesus proposed truth, but He didn't impose it."

The speaker pointed out that Jesus didn't force Himself or His gospel on others. He offered it like crazy, but He didn't impose it. He said anyone who was thirsty could come to Him and drink and receive streams of living water (John 7:37-38). Jesus didn't restrain people in straitjackets and pour His water down their throats. He didn't impose His love, His truth, or His life. He *offered* it. He proposed a new way to live in total dependence on God. He proposed humility, freedom, and forgiveness for whoever would believe in Him and follow Him.

As His followers, we can learn from His way. Especially during the Christmas season, we can take a humble posture as we go to holiday gatherings or parties. We can walk in the door prepared to listen with understanding. We explain our perspectives, but we don't get angry when others see things from a different point of view.

Just last night I wanted to make a point and get my husband to agree with my opinion. I went too far. I wanted him in a straitjacket so I could pour my truth water down his throat. It was over the littlest thing like what noises are annoying to most people. Don't laugh, I bet some of your fights are silly too. Right?

Let's learn to propose the way Jesus did. To offer a thirsty world the best Water—whether it is those in our own families, our communities, or even strangers on social media. When others prefer not to drink our water, we don't have to keep pushing our way. Instead, we continue to freely offer and live love . . . especially when we don't see eye to eye.

I hope you'll remember today that Jesus is proposing to you. As we remember His birth, remember His life as well. He invites you to drink His satisfying water as you walk through the ups and downs of life today. Say *yes*!

Dear Lord, I want to follow You. I long to know You and emulate You in my understanding of truth but also in how I communicate my belief. You are the Truth. I long to drink Your living water and offer it to a thirsty world. Show me how to do it Your way. I humble myself before You asking You to fill me up. In Jesus' name I pray, amen.

QUESTIONS FOR REFLECTION

What parties or events will be the most challenging to attend due to strained relationships or uncomfortable conversations?

What will help prepare your heart with humility as you interact with others at holiday gatherings?

Is there a specific area where God is calling you to take the posture of child and propose truth instead of impose it?

A PRACTICAL APPROACH

Here are some thoughts to consider on humility:

- As you think through your plans with family or friends, does it always have to be your way? Ask a family member or friend how he or she would like to do something.
- Do a word study on all the times humble or humility is used in Scripture using websites like Biblegateway.com or the YouVersion app on a phone or tablet. Look for common threads or personal applications to help shape your patterns of thought toward humility.

Day 14

WITHHOLDING

What shall we say about such wonderful things as these? If God is for us,
who can ever be against us? Since he did not spare even his own Son but
gave him up for us all, won't he also give us everything else?
~ Romans 8:31-32

For the LORD God is our sun and our shield.
He gives us grace and glory.
The LORD will withhold no good thing
from those who do what is right.
~ Psalm 84:11

Silence can speak louder than any words spoken. It can communicate neglect and a lack of care. It can do great harm to people we love. When I hear people tell about their childhood hurts, they often refer to what wasn't done. They weren't told they were loved, people didn't come to their school events, or some other important thing they needed wasn't given. Withholding can cause deep pain. I've noticed that God is as concerned about our inaction as He is with our action.

Some examples from Scripture that have popped out in my daily readings include:

- Eli withheld discipline from his sons and it cost him dearly.
- David failed to give justice to his daughter when she was raped.
- King Amaziah did a lot of good things, but he didn't get rid of idol worship completely.

Scripture is full of examples of people whose wrong behaviors brought consequences that echoed for generations. It helps me remember that my choices matter. They affect not only those close to me now, but they ripple into the future for the grandchildren I haven't met yet. This weighty truth encourages me to pursue wisdom and truth in my words, actions, and habits. However, I sometimes forget that while what I do matters, what I choose not to do also has an impact.

As we are thinking about our rituals and relationships at Christmas, we must evaluate our decisions of omission as much as our acts of commission. Some areas that come to mind when I think about the dangers of inaction are:

- **Not expressing love with my words and actions.** Children especially need constant assurance and reminders that they are loved and treasured. I've found that husbands and friends like to hear it often too. It nurtures deep relationships. Christmas is a time when we shouldn't withhold our blessing and love, whether shown through words or actions.
- **Thinking grateful thoughts but not speaking them.** Life is so busy, especially during the holidays. I think often about how thankful I am for meals, small acts of kindness, grace given for mistakes, or prayers offered on my behalf. Yet in the crazy rush I sometimes withhold expressing my gratitude.

These are just two examples where I need to be on guard against withholding. I don't want my busyness or laziness to keep me from doing things I know are important. Of course, we will never get it all right. Sometimes we forget things and miss opportunities. That's what I love about Scripture—it reminds us that even the great men and women of God made mistakes a lot.

But we can learn from their sins of omission and be inspired to express our love, discipline our children, and not withhold justice from those who are counting on us. Proverbs 3:27 says, "Do not withhold good from those who deserve it / when it's in your power to help them."

While busyness is sometimes the reason I withhold, at other times my people-pleasing tendencies are the culprit. We might withhold for fear the person will think our offering is silly, unnecessary, or not appropriate. Yet time has proved that when I listen to God and go ahead with what He is asking of me, He blesses it. That doesn't mean it's never complicated or without opposition. Recently I felt the Holy Spirit leading me to gather some high school girls I had discipled since they were in sixth grade. I wanted it to be a special night of blessing, but some wires got crossed and feelings got hurt. I questioned whether I had heard correctly from God in taking initiative for the night and hated that someone got hurt because of my actions. I will admit that in the midst of the situation, I wished I had just brushed off the idea and saved myself the drama. Yet, at the end of the day, it was a very special evening.

God worked out the problems, caused growth in my life in navigating tender relationships, and really encouraged some of the gals as they prepare to leave for college next year! Withholding may seem easier, but aren't we glad God didn't withhold on us? He sent His one and only Son so that we might have a restored relationship with the Father!

Romans 8:32 tells us that "since he did not spare even his own Son . . . won't He also give us everything else?" God doesn't withhold His affection, provision, or forgiveness. He lavishly pours it out. As we stay close to Him, we can identify areas where we might be withholding and make changes to pour out blessings on those around us.

God, You didn't withhold Your own Son. It's why we celebrate! Please help me to be like You. Even my most precious relationship or possession is available to be given up to You. Help me to hear You clearly to see where I may be withholding in relationships. Help me to speak truth and show love when and where You call me. In Jesus' name I pray, amen.

QUESTIONS FOR REFLECTION

What have you been holding back for fear of how it might be received?

What thought or idea has been playing at the corners of your mind, but you've brushed it aside?

Where might the Lord be calling you to express words or actions of blessings in the lives of others?

A PRACTICAL APPROACH

Take a moment today to write a note, make a call, send a text, or find another way to express love and blessing in someone else's life.

Day 15

FORGIVENESS

"Come now, let's settle this,"
    says the LORD.
"Though your sins are like scarlet,
    I will make them as white as snow.
Though they are red like crimson,
    I will make them as white as wool."
~ Isaiah 1:18

For a child is born to us,
    a son is given to us.
The government will rest on his shoulders.
    And he will be called:
Wonderful Counselor, Mighty God,
    Everlasting Father, Prince of Peace.
His government and its peace
    will never end.
He will rule with fairness and justice from the throne of his ancestor David
    for all eternity.
The passionate commitment of the LORD *of Heaven's Armies*
    will make this happen!
~ Isaiah 9:6-7

Christmas celebrations bring together coworkers, friends, and family members, and it can be a time when old wounds reemerge. We see someone and remember a snarky comment, hurtful post on social media, or maybe even a bigger betrayal. At this time of year when we celebrate Christ's birth, we rejoice that He came to earth to show us how to live but also to pay the price for our sins to give us a great gift—forgiveness. In the Lord's Prayer found in Matthew 6, we find these words,

> "Give us today the food we need,
>   and forgive us our sins,
>   as we have forgiven those who sin against us."
> (vv. 11-12)

Just as we need food every day, we also must receive and extend forgiveness on a daily basis. Think now about that person whom you will see this holiday season that you would rather not. Maybe he or she makes passive-aggressive comments, brings up your faults in public, or just makes you feel small by ignoring you. It's difficult to revise our feelings when they invade our thoughts and spill out into our words. How can we truly forgive? Only as we receive God's forgiveness through His Son, Jesus, can we overflow forgiveness on those around us. When I am practically trying to work out forgiveness in my life over small disappointments or recurring wounds, I have discovered a helpful tool in yielding to God to do the heavy lifting of forgiveness.

In his book titled *Forgiveness: Finding Peace Through Letting Go*, Adam Hamilton shared a very practical acronym to help us become professional forgivers (pp. 73–76). When you feel the tension rise, RAP up the best gift you can give to others (and yourself).

R—Remember your own shortcomings.

Nobody's perfect, and when we take off our Pharisee glasses we will see that we make mistakes too. It makes it easier to see our offenders more clearly as one sinner forgiving another sinner.

A—Assume the best of people.

We often default to thinking the worst. We assume the motives and intent of others, and we can even blow balloons in our heads by reading more into someone's tone, posture, or comment than was ever intended. Assuming the best keeps us from inflating a situation.

P—Pray for them.

People who are unkind sometimes have a deeper hurt beneath the surface. Ask God to bless and help them. In Matthew 5:44, Jesus said, "But I say, love your enemies! Pray for those who persecute you!" A great way to celebrate His birth would be to obey this command He gave us.

I have found rehearsing the truths behind these three letters a great way to get on the other side of our pain. When we are stuck in bitterness, we can't encourage those around us. Our focus is inward rather than outward. Christmas is a time to think of Christ and others rather than dwell on ourselves.

We can't forgive others in our own strength. Only Christ can do the transforming work of supernatural forgiveness in us. I liken trying to forgive on my own to using a hairdryer without plugging it in. I can get frustrated that it isn't working, but all I need to do is put the plug into the socket to actualize the power source. In the same way, Christ is our forgiveness power source.

He is the Wonderful Counselor, Mighty God, Everlasting Father, and Prince of Peace. He will rule with fairness. He will sort out justice with perfect clarity. As you rub shoulders with people who have hurt you in the past, I hope you'll plug into Christ. He came to forgive! He wants you to live free from bitterness. One of the reasons I'm not a huge fan of rap music is that the songs seem to say the same lines over and over. When it comes to our forgiveness RAP, we may need to rehearse it over and over again

- as we get ready and prepare to walk into a place where we'll encounter those who have hurt us,
- when we see the person across the room talking and laughing,
- as we make small talk, or
- on the car ride home as we rehearse each word exchanged.

By transforming our patterns of thought, we'll find new attitudes of compassion replacing our feelings of anger and sadness. No matter what is happening in your life, remember to RAP up grace and find God's peace inside!

God, I don't want to live in bitterness that will poison my soul. I am bringing all my hurt to You. Help me to rediscover the humanity of my offenders, knowing that I make a lot of mistakes too. Lord, please ease any anxiety I feel about interacting with difficult people. Help me to share Your love from a pure heart that only You can give me. Free me so that I can be an agent of Your freedom this holiday season. In Jesus' name I pray, amen.

QUESTIONS FOR REFLECTION

Is there anyone you think of negatively on a regular basis?

How can you apply the RAP idea to a personal situation in your life?

When you think of Christ turning all your sins as white as snow, how does His forgiveness bring freedom for you?

A PRACTICAL APPROACH

Consider these points on forgiveness:

- Is there someone to whom you need to apologize? Christmas is a great reason to approach him or her humbly and seek forgiveness and reconciliation!
- Write out the RAP acronym on a notecard where you can see it, and make a habit of keeping short accounts with those you love over the holidays.

Day 16

THE LANGUAGES
OF LOVE

*Dear friends, let us continue to love one another, for love comes from God.
Anyone who loves is a child of God and knows God. But anyone who does
not love does not know God, for God is love.*

*God showed how much he loved us by sending his one and only Son
into the world so that we might have eternal life through him. This is real
love—not that we loved God, but that he loved us and sent his Son as a
sacrifice to take away our sins.*

*Dear friends, since God loved us that much, we surely ought to love
each other. No one has ever seen God. But if we love each other, God lives in
us, and his love is brought to full expression in us.*
~ 1 John 4:7-12

My parents live in Texas, and my husband's family is in Canada.
Since we live in Ohio, holiday traveling can be tricky. In
addition, Christmas is a very busy time for people in ministry; it's
not hard to understand why we often end up celebrating Christmas
without extended family. Over the last twenty years, our family has
typically gathered with my longtime mentor and friend, Deb, and
her family. Both she and her husband give generously of their time,
talents, and treasures; and they spoil my family with wisdom and
gifts. When it comes time to find a special gift for her family at the
holidays, I usually feel anxiety because I'm not good at picking out
gifts. I don't know what to get her that will convey my appreciation
and love.

About ten years ago, I found myself stressing once again as the Christmas season approached. I thought about the beautifully wrapped gifts under Deb's tree with Spoelstra tags on them. I racked my brain to think of something good to give Deb. God brought to my mind Gary Chapman's marriage book, *The 5 Love Languages*. That book gave me great insight in realizing that not everyone receives love in the same way. While working as a marriage counselor for more than thirty years, Gary identified the five love languages people show and accept as

- Words of Affirmation,
- Quality Time,
- Receiving Gifts,
- Acts of Service, and
- Physical Touch.

I considered my dear friend Deb. Knowing her as I do, I wondered if the language of Quality Time might be her primary way of feeling valued and loved. So I decided my three girls and I would take her, her daughter, and her daughter-in-law out for a special lunch. We went to a tearoom that had a Christmas boutique and lots of decorations, and we had a lovely lunch. I brought along a few questions that we all had to answer—sharing our highlights from the year, as well as Christmas memories from the past. We enjoyed it so much that we have made the lunch and the questions an annual tradition.

For more than a decade now, I haven't had to stress about choosing a gift for Deb. We all look forward to this special time eating, laughing, and taking a break from the Christmas craziness to value the people we love. As we think about focusing on rituals, relationships, and rest this December, we can consider the people God has placed in our lives. One way to do this is to ask the question, How can we express our love toward others in a way that is meaningful to them?

When I first discovered the concept of love languages, I began to see that my tendency to love others is the way I prefer to be loved. My primary love language is Acts of Service. I feel valued when my husband changes a light bulb or fills up my car with gas. When friends serve alongside me in ministry or run an errand for me, I sense God's love through them. However, I have found that my husband's love language is different. While he still appreciates clean socks in his drawer or a meal prepared, he really feels treasured when I hold his hand or speak affirming words to him.

Today's passage from 1 John tells us that real love is not that we loved God, but that He loved us and sacrificially sent His Son. John goes on to say, "Dear friends, since God loved us that much, we surely ought to love each other. No one has ever seen God. But if we love each other, God lives in us, and his love is brought to full expression in us" (1 John 4:11-12).

Wow . . . did you catch that? When we love each other, God's love is brought to full expression in us. One of the ways we can love each other well is to keep the love languages in mind. Instead of hoping our loved ones are just like us, we can acknowledge that God made all of us unique. We have different personalities, birth orders, and ways we prefer to receive love. As you focus on relationships this month, look for ways to discover your friends' and family members' love languages. In doing this, you'll find God's love finding full expression in you!

Lord, I don't want to assume everyone else is like me. Help me to value the diversity and uniqueness of those You have put in my life to love. Whether I am showing love to my family, friends, coworkers, or neighbors, I long to be an expression of Your love in me. Thank You for sending your Son sacrificially. Give me creative ways to show Your love to others this holiday season. In Jesus' name I pray, amen.

QUESTIONS FOR REFLECTION

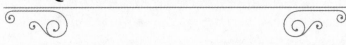

Which love language is your primary way of receiving love?

How does knowing that loving others brings God's love to full expression encourage you?

To whom is God calling you to show His love this week?

A PRACTICAL APPROACH

Identify a "Deb" in your life. Is there someone who has loved you well for many years? Think of someone who has invested time, talents, and treasures in your life. Then spend some time identifying your best guess regarding that person's love language. Here are a few ideas you could implement to express love:

Words of Affirmation. Write a note or send a text or email expressing some of the things you appreciate.

Quality Time. Plan an outing where you get to spend some unhurried time together.

Receiving Gifts. Buy something you know the person wouldn't purchase for himself or herself and would bring joy.

Acts of Service. Identify a way to help in a practical way, such as wrapping gifts, running errands, or bringing a meal.

Physical Touch. This one can be a little tricky when it's outside of marriage. While physical touch isn't necessarily sexual, be sure to have proper boundaries as you give a high five, hug, or pat on the back! Make sure the touch is welcomed.

Day 17

BEING NEIGHBORLY

One day an expert in religious law stood up to test Jesus by asking him this question: "Teacher, what should I do to inherit eternal life?"

Jesus replied, "What does the law of Moses say? How do you read it?"

The man answered, "You must love the LORD your God with all your heart, all your soul, all your strength, and all your mind." And, "Love your neighbor as yourself."

"Right!" Jesus told him. "Do this and you will live!"

The man wanted to justify his actions, so he asked Jesus, "And who is my neighbor?"

Jesus replied with a story: "A Jewish man was traveling from Jerusalem down to Jericho, and he was attacked by bandits. They stripped him of his clothes, beat him up, and left him half dead beside the road.

"By chance a priest came along. But when he saw the man lying there, he crossed to the other side of the road and passed him by. A Temple assistant walked over and looked at him lying there, but he also passed by on the other side.

"Then a despised Samaritan came along, and when he saw the man, he felt compassion for him. Going over to him, the Samaritan soothed his wounds with olive oil and wine and bandaged them. Then he put the man on his own donkey and took him to an inn, where he took care of him. The next day he handed the innkeeper two silver coins, telling him, 'Take care of this man. If his bill runs higher than this, I'll pay you the next time I'm here.'

"Now which of these three would you say was a neighbor to the man who was attacked by bandits?" Jesus asked.

The man replied, "The one who showed him mercy."

Then Jesus said, "Yes, now go and do the same."

~ Luke 10:25-37

I spent an hour this afternoon at my neighbor's house listening to the adventures of a new mom. I had a looming to-do list and had spent the morning babysitting for a friend. Yet when she texted me and asked me to drop by, I remembered those early years with my first child. It can be lonely at home all day. We had a great time catching up since winter seems to distance our neighborly relationship.

The whole concept of neighboring has changed since I was a child. Technology has created the ability to watch television nonstop. We don't have to wait for certain days or times to watch our favorite shows. Garage doors go up and come down with a click of a button so that we rarely encounter our neighbors.

From our reading today we heard the command to love our neighbors as ourselves. This means that we treat them the way we would want to be treated if we were in their shoes. Of course this doesn't mean we can respond with a yes to every invitation. Some neighborhood associations have parties, cookie exchanges, or a special night for children during the holidays. We can't go to everything and invest in everyone or we would have no time for the rest we will be reading about in our last ten devotions.

However, when we see a need or receive a personal ask for something, we need to go back to the Golden Rule and ask ourselves, "How would I want to be treated in this situation?" The biblical books of Romans, Galatians, and James reiterate the important truth of living by the second greatest commandment. Galatians 5:14 says, "For the whole law can be summed up in this one command: 'Love your neighbor as yourself.'"

When we act in a way that is truly loving toward others, the law isn't necessary. Love isn't jealous, dishonest, dishonoring, or adulterous. The commandments center around these types of prohibitions. We learn from the parable of the good Samaritan that our neighbor doesn't have to live near us, but let's start there. Who are the people with houses that surround yours? Do you know them? Have you treated them the way you would want to be treated?

For many years when my husband and I were steeped in ministry at a large church, we helped run many programs. We spent a lot of hours at the church building attending events, weekly meetings, and services. Our children attended private school, so we had even fewer opportunities to connect with families in our neighborhood. When my husband felt the call to plant a church, we knew this was one thing we wanted to change. We didn't want to be so busy doing church stuff that we didn't have time to know our neighbors.

As my children entered the local schools, I met many other parents. We began attending community events and inviting neighbors over for dinner or game nights. After nine years, I can tell you that we have deep relationships with many of those who live around us. At times we have invited neighbors to our small group parties or special events at our church. A couple across the street emailed us after we invited them to a Bible study when they seemed to really enjoy our small group Christmas party. They said they treasured our friendship but weren't really interested in church and wanted to know if we could still hang out. We affirmed them and wanted them to know they weren't a project. They were friends.

Of course for those we love, we want them to know Jesus. We believe He is the only way that leads to peace for this life and the next. Yet, at the same time, we don't want our loved ones to feel as if we are "selling" Jesus, and if they don't want to buy we are moving on.

Beyond those who live near us are other people such as the Samaritan on the road. These individuals are those we notice are hurting whether they are strangers, coworkers, family members, or friends. They need help—often physical help. While we must be wise about vetting a person or situation, some people truly have circumstances like the man in the parable who was mistreated.

In our comfortable lives we cannot forget

- women who have been trafficked,
- children who have been abused,
- spouses who have been battered,
- immigrants in need of food and shelter,
- parents who have lost their jobs,
- individuals with health problems that bring medical bills and unemployment, and
- the working poor who labor diligently but struggle to make ends meet.

The trials of this life are many. How would we want to be treated if we were in these types of situations? I know I would be on the lookout for mercy and someone who didn't look overly stressed or busy. As we put ourselves in the place of the good Samaritan, how would we react? Would we assume someone else would take care of the injured person or would we stop and get involved?

Take a moment right now to think of your actual neighbors. Is anyone in need? Maybe no one is lying out in the road physically, but he or she has real spiritual, emotional, or physical needs that you could help with this Christmas.

God, help me to see the needs around me. I want to know how You are calling me to love my neighbor as myself. Show me the places You are calling me to invest my time and resources in relationships with others. Thank You for calling your followers to help the wounded and for explaining what it means to really love our neighbors. In Jesus' name I pray, amen.

QUESTIONS FOR REFLECTION

How well do you know the people who live near you? How might you form a better relationship with them?

Where is God calling you to love your neighbors with a whole heart?

What is one practical expression of love you can show to someone who is suffering during the holiday season?

A PRACTICAL APPROACH

Consider the following as opportunities to help your fellow neighbor:

- Invite a few neighbors over without asking them to bring anything—no food, no gift exchange, and so on. Just get to know each other.
- Prayerfully consider someone in your sphere of influence who has been mistreated or is in need of help. Ask the Holy Spirit to guide you in meeting a practical need.
- Set aside a portion of your Christmas budget for helping others. Get your family involved in looking around for those who are suffering and ways you can help meet needs.

Day 18

SPIRITUAL GIFTS

So let's not get tired of doing what is good. At just the right time we will reap a harvest of blessing if we don't give up. Therefore, whenever we have the opportunity, we should do good to everyone—especially to those in the family of faith.
~ Galatians 6:9-10

God has given each of you a gift from his great variety of spiritual gifts. Use them well to serve one another.
~ 1 Peter 4:10

God works in different ways, but it is the same God who does the work in all of us.
     A spiritual gift is given to each of us so we can help each other.
~ 1 Corinthians 12:6-7

Living in a small home with a husband and four kids leaves little space for clutter. My husband and I have always had a thing about excess toys, stuffed animals, and junk—especially when our kids were younger. Each year, before Christmas, we would put a laundry basket in the center of the playroom and tell the kids they had to fill it with items to donate before we would introduce any new toys as presents. As I reflect on the years of gifts that have been exchanged in our family, I have no idea what became of most of that stuff. The gifts were expressions of love that brought temporary joy with the lasting effect of fond memories.

Can you think of a meaningful gift you have received? God is a gift-giver too—but His gifts never end up in a resale shop, at the bottom of a landfill, or in a laundry basket to be donated to charity. We serve a generous God who gives us good and perfect gifts! God's gifts are not only physical but also spiritual.

As we focus on relationships and valuing people at Christmas, we remember that the Lord equips us to serve each other in our local church bodies. While it is important to reach out to neighbors and friends and remember teachers, postal workers, and coworkers, we must not overlook our brothers and sisters in Christ. God loves it when we encourage and serve each other.

In the midst of the holiday season, we can be especially intentional in using our spiritual gifts to bless those in our church family. Spiritual gifts are not just for pastors, leaders, or mature believers. Everyone who has chosen to follow Christ receives a special ability to serve others.

The Christmas gifts we've purchased for our kids over the years were for their own personal enjoyment. They played with plastic dishes, rammed remote control cars into the couch, and wore the clothes and shoes they desired. But the spiritual gifts that God gives are not meant to make us feel good—though they certainly do. They are meant to edify and build up others in the body. And every gift is important.

Recognizing that people use different terms and definitions for the gifts found in Romans 12:6-8; Ephesians 4:11; 1 Peter 4:10-11; and 1 Corinthians 12:8-11, here is one compilation of the gifts:

Administration	Giving
Apostleship	Healing
Discernment	Interpretation of Tongues
Evangelism	Knowledge
Exhortation/Encouragement	Leadership
Faith	Mercy/Compassion

Miracles	Teaching
Pastor/Shepherd	Tongues
Prophecy	Wisdom
Serving/Ministering	

As you read over this list, what is one gift that you might possess? Discovering our gifts can help us understand how God wants to use us to build up the rest of the body of Christ. Christmas is a great time to use our gifts. Can you think of one way you might use your gift or gifts this week to bless someone else?

Christmas can be an especially stressful time for pastors. They often plan extra services to celebrate Christ's birth. Children's ministry workers and youth leaders plan special activities to help students understand the true meaning of Christmas. A word of encouragement, help with a project, or just showing up can be a way to love and support those who serve consistently all year long.

With relationships a key element in biblical celebration, serving and connecting should be a priority. As you think about the people in your church family, be sure to take a moment to prayerfully consider how you might be a blessing to someone else in your community of worship.

Lord, I am so thankful for my church family. I praise You for being an amazing Gift-giver! Thank You for sending Your Son to die for me. While my church is full of imperfect people like me, I'm so glad that I don't have to feel alone in my walk with You. Help me to use the gift You have given me to serve others in my local community. I don't want to grow weary in doing good, so help me to use my gift with Your strength. In Jesus' name I pray, amen.

QUESTIONS FOR REFLECTION

What is your spiritual gift?

What is one small way you can serve someone in your church this week?

How has someone in your church encouraged you recently? How can you show encouragement and thanks back to that individual?

A PRACTICAL APPROACH

Consider the following as opportunities to help those within your church:

- Offer to help serve in the nursery for the Christmas Eve service. (Your children's ministry director will cry happy tears!)
- Take a meal to someone who is struggling with a physical or emotional ailment this Christmas.
- Write a note of encouragement to someone you have noticed serving all year as a greeter, worship team member, Sunday school teacher, or anyone the Lord brings to mind. Tell the person specifically what you appreciate about his or her service.

Day 19

THE LEAST OF THESE

"But when the Son of Man comes in his glory, and all the angels with him, then he will sit upon his glorious throne. All the nations will be gathered in his presence, and he will separate the people as a shepherd separates the sheep from the goats. He will place the sheep at his right hand and the goats at his left.

"Then the King will say to those on his right, 'Come, you who are blessed by my Father, inherit the Kingdom prepared for you from the creation of the world. For I was hungry, and you fed me. I was thirsty, and you gave me a drink. I was a stranger, and you invited me into your home. I was naked, and you gave me clothing. I was sick, and you cared for me. I was in prison, and you visited me.'

"Then these righteous ones will reply, 'Lord, when did we ever see you hungry and feed you? Or thirsty and give you something to drink? Or a stranger and show you hospitality? Or naked and give you clothing? When did we ever see you sick or in prison and visit you?'

"And the King will say, 'I tell you the truth, when you did it to one of the least of these my brothers and sisters, you were doing it to me!'"
~ Matthew 25:31-40

God went all out to announce and celebrate the birth of His Son with a multitude of angels. I love that the audience was a group of shepherds. It wasn't government officials, religious leaders, or those who considered themselves important. Instead it was a group of humble shepherds caring for animals.

Jesus came to earth to save us from sin but also to teach us how to live. He taught His disciples that God values humility, kindness, and reaching out to those in need. He clearly communicated that He is coming again. We celebrate His birth at Christmas and remember that it was a first coming. When He returns it will be in glory with all the angels alongside Him.

Until that day comes, Jesus told us that caring for the needs of others is valuable to Him. He claimed that when we do it for the least person, we are doing it for Him. I notice that Christ mentioned both physical and emotional needs in our Scripture reading today:

- hunger
- thirst
- hospitality
- clothing
- a personal visit

These are tangible ways that we can show the love of God. It is possible to become jaded and lose compassion for people. Sometimes bad choices have landed individuals in places of need. Other times circumstances have imposed hardship upon them. As I mentioned previously, a close friend of mine works for a local agency that runs an Adopt-a-Family Christmas program that offers families the opportunity to sign up to receive Christmas presents. Last year, when all the gifts had been delivered, my friend got a call from a mom saying she had not received the presents for her children. This mom was getting nervous with Christmas only a few days away.

After doing some digging, my friend found that the person who had been given that particular family had decided not to purchase gifts. For whatever reason she had personally deemed them not "needy" enough and decided to do something for another family who seemed more worthy. My friend stepped into action and made sure this mother, who was signed up for the program, got gifts for her children. We all must make decisions about where and how we are to share the resources He has given us. As we do this we must remember the command of Christ and not become cynical about how worthy people must be to receive.

It is important to do a little fact-checking or research to be sure we aren't being scammed or contributing to an addiction. Over the years, my pastor-husband has had to discern through several situations of need. As a youth pastor, many years ago, he found that some people just randomly call churches asking for help. When we don't know the person or aren't sure about the story, we can look for red flags, ask for references, and seek the Holy Spirit to give us wisdom.

At times we have been what we call "beautiful fools." Sometimes we have given to strangers because God told us to give. In hindsight, we've learned that a person may be lying or living off the naivety of spiritual people to get something. However, with the words of Jesus we read today, wouldn't you rather err on the side of generosity? We would hate to deny a true need because of those who take advantage. I would rather be a beautiful fool from time to time than become numb toward the needs of others.

During the holidays, many organizations run great programs. They often have more experience in discerning true needs. The Salvation Army has a great reputation for fiscal responsibility and years of service to the poor in our communities. Look for agencies with longevity, good leadership, and personal connections.

God doesn't call us to give just to those in our own circles. Most people are inclined to give gifts to their own families. Jesus said, "You parents—if your children ask for a loaf of bread, do you give them a stone instead? Or if they ask for a fish, do you give them a snake? Of course not! So if you sinful people know how to give good gifts to your children, how much more will your heavenly Father give good gifts to those who ask him. Do to others whatever you would like them to do to you. This is the essence of all that is taught in the law and the prophets" (Matthew 7:9-12).

As we practice the Golden Rule by treating others the way we would like to be treated, we must put ourselves in the shoes of those who are suffering. Even if bad choices landed us in prison, would we want to be visited? Even if we managed our money poorly, would we want something to eat today? Even if we struggled with addiction, would we want compassion and help?

Christ's call to help meet the physical and emotional needs of others as we await His return rings so true during Christmas. When we get involved helping those with needs during the holiday season, it often whets our appetites to continue reaching out throughout the year.

God, open my eyes to see those who are suffering. Use me as Your hands and feet to provide food, clothing, shelter, and relationship to others. Help me to remember that I am doing it for You. I may never be thanked or understand the true nature of the circumstances. Lord, show me how to give like You—generously, sacrificially, and freely. In Jesus' name I pray, amen.

QUESTIONS FOR REFLECTION

Is there anyone you know right now who is struggling to pay bills, provide for children, or buy groceries? How can you help them? If you do not have funds, are there other ways you can be of help?

What organizations have you partnered with in the past in your community or across the globe to provide tangible help to others? What did you learn from them, and how can you incorporate that into your everyday life?

Have you ever struggled with becoming cynical about providing for others because of those who take advantage of help? What daily reminder can you give yourself of what Christ asks of you?

A PRACTICAL APPROACH

Consider the following when thinking of ways to help those in need:

- Gather a group of friends from church (Bible study or small group) and spend a night serving together. You can adopt a family to shop for, volunteer together for an organization, or find a way to meet the needs of others tangibly.
- Pray for those in other countries. God hears our prayers. Use a resource such as the books *Operation World* (for adults) or *Windows on the World* (for children) as a guide to pray for those around the globe.
- Look for ways to help others beyond the Christmas season: free medical clinics, tutoring programs, and shelters need volunteers and financial support all year long!

Day 20

PEOPLE AND PATIENCE

Brothers and sisters, we urge you to warn those who are lazy. Encourage
those who are timid. Take tender care of those who are weak. Be patient
with everyone.

See that no one pays back evil for evil, but always try to do good to each
other and to all people.

Always be joyful. Never stop praying. Be thankful in all
circumstances, for this is God's will for you who belong to Christ Jesus.
~ 1 Thessalonians 5:14-18

During the holiday season, we encounter all sorts of people. In the array of coworkers, family, friends, and strangers whom we will be alongside, we will find individuals with many different postures. Some may be in need of encouragement while others need tender care. The holidays can be times of great joy where we celebrate Jesus and the opportunity to connect with family members. For others, the season can highlight the pain of strained relationships, debilitating health conditions, or the absence after the death of a loved one.

Paul told the church at Thessalonica to take tender care of those who are weak. Who in your life is heavy with grief, pain, or difficulty this Christmas season? How might God be calling you to take tender care of them? Whether it's a kind word, a meal, a thoughtful gift, or time spent together, ask God how you might express His love to them this season.

The sentence that stands out most in today's passage is this one: **Be patient with everyone.**

Patience is not my strong suit. I often move at two speeds: fast and faster. Slow traffic, delayed decisions, or kids who don't come out right after practice can make me agitated fairly quickly. I am not a fan of waiting. In the hustle and bustle of the busy holiday season, what if we slowed down? What if we were truly patient with everyone, including:

- the clerk at the store who seems to be taking his or her time with your purchases;
- the child who isn't ready to go when you are;
- the spouse who comes home late from work (Maybe your spouse was buying you a gift?);
- the person with the words *in-law* at the end of your relationship who does things so differently than you do; or
- the coworker who isn't pulling his or her weight, leaving a lot on your plate?

Who else would you add to this list? Is the Lord calling you to show patience toward someone? This verse leaves no room for exceptions. God asks us to be patient with others as He is patient with us. God sent His Son to earth to redeem us. He understands our bent toward sin, and He made a way to bring us back into relationship with Him. The timeline for both His first and second comings is not slow but reveals His patience: "The Lord isn't really being slow about his promise, as some people think. No, he is being patient for your sake. He does not want anyone to be destroyed, but wants everyone to repent" (2 Peter 3:9).

God waits patiently on us to repent and come back to Him. He also asks us to be patient with one another. In 1 Thessalonians 5:15-16, Paul gave the church a few more instructions to help them relate with each other:

- Never pay back evil for evil.
- Always be joyful.
- Never stop praying.
- Be thankful in all circumstances.

These practices will be helpful postures in tapping into God's patience and expressing it to others. As we've seen over these last ten days, relationships are vital to biblical celebration. In the midst of our Christmas season we can treasure people. Only God's Word and people will last forever. The beautiful decorations, sweet treats, and fancy cards are wonderful, but only the people themselves are eternal. Let's give them the gift of patience as we rub shoulders in the coming days and weeks.

Lord, thank You for being so patient with me. Lord, You know my struggles to show patience toward that certain person. Give me Your strength by the Holy Spirit to love others and treasure them. Help me to prioritize people above schedules, stuff, and circumstances. In Jesus' name I pray, amen.

QUESTIONS FOR REFLECTION

How has God been patient with you recently?

Who is the Lord calling you to be patient with today? How can you show them that they are a priority to you?

Is there someone who needs tender care from you this week? What can you do to provide that care?

A PRACTICAL APPROACH

Consider the following when thinking of the needs of others:

- Reach out to someone who has lost a loved one this year and let that person know you remember them and are thinking of them in their grief.
- The next time you are getting impatient with someone, count to ten before you react. Then ask God to give you His patience before responding in any way.

REST

Day 21

SABBATH

Passover: *"For seven days you must present special gifts to the LORD. On the seventh day the people must again stop all their ordinary work to observe an official day for holy assembly."*
~ Leviticus 23:8

The Festival of Trumpets: *"Give the following instructions to the people of Israel. On the first day of the appointed month in early autumn, you are to observe a day of complete rest. It will be an official day for holy assembly, a day commemorated with loud blasts of a trumpet. You must do no ordinary work on that day. Instead, you are to present special gifts to the LORD."*
~ Leviticus 23:24-25

The Day of Atonement: *"You must not do any work at all! This is a permanent law for you, and it must be observed from generation to generation wherever you live. This will be a Sabbath day of complete rest for you, and on that day you must deny yourselves. This day of rest will begin at sundown on the ninth day of the month and extend until sundown on the tenth day."*
~ Leviticus 23:31-32

The Festival of Shelters: *"For seven days you must present special gifts to the LORD. The eighth day is another holy day on which you present your special gifts to the LORD. This will be a solemn occasion, and no ordinary work may be done that day."*
~ Leviticus 23:36

R-E-S-T

Do these four letters describe your month of December? It certainly isn't the first word that comes to my mind. Yet as we look at biblical celebrations such as Passover, the Festival of Trumpets, the Day of Atonement, and the Festival of Shelters, we find the concept of Sabbath to be an important one. God was very specific in the verses we read from Leviticus today to instruct the people to include rest in their celebrations. Rest includes

- stopping all ordinary work,
- gathering for holy assembly,
- complete rest,
- presenting the Lord with special gifts,
- denying self, and
- solemn occasion.

God created us, and He knows we need to stop and remember. We must break from ordinary routines so that we can commune with Him in celebration and commemoration. These Israelite holidays were meant to help the people remember what the Lord had done for them:

- He delivered them from Egypt.
- He atoned for their sin.
- He led them safely through the wilderness.

The sacred celebrations were a time to stop and remember. At Christmas we do a similar thing in that we incorporate new rituals, connect with people, and stop our ordinary routines to think about what the Lord has done. He sent His Son to earth.

John 3:16 reminds us why He did this: "For this is how God loved the world: He gave his one and only Son, so that everyone who believes in him will not perish but have eternal life." That is why we celebrate. However, we can't just stop ordinary work and fill it with new kinds of busyness. Instead, we are to plan for times of complete rest.

I'm not good at resting. I can write about it, but I struggle to do it. Resting sometimes makes me feel guilty and unproductive. Our culture doesn't value rest. It values leisure but not necessarily rest. There is a difference. The biblical definition of rest is not escaping. It is not endless hours of staring at a screen or being entertained. Biblical rest brings us closer to the Lord and nourishes our souls.

People are wired so differently that some things that are restful for me might not be restful for you. So we must prayerfully pursue rest. One question we can ask is this: "Does this restful encounter bring me closer to God?" When my body is refreshed from sleep, I find myself less irritated. Fatigue can leave me vulnerable to attacks of the enemy. So, in a way, physical rest can bring me closer to God.

Other activities that are restful for me include

- taking a walk,
- seeing God's creation in nature,
- reading a good book or novel,
- reading the Bible,
- prayer,
- working on a puzzle,
- writing in my journal,
- just lying on the couch thinking, and
- having a conversation with someone I love.

My husband would not find several of the things on my list restful. Instead, he might prefer to play a sports game, listen to music, or interact with a group of people. Introverts and extroverts might find different types of things restful. In the past year I have tried to be more intentional about rest. I've put it in my schedule and dedicated some days to putting away all electronic devices (including my phone) to rest from "notifications." I found myself still trying to be productive in my rest. I would read a commentary I know I will need for a future book. I'd take a walk to get in some exercise. Someone recently shared with me that true rest produces nothing.

For those who struggle with worshipping at the altar of productivity, that's a tough one. How about you? We are not under the Old Testament law, and most of us don't observe the Jewish festivals. However, we can learn from the example of biblical celebration that rest is an important aspect of our faith. We don't want to rush through Christmas, checking off our lists and just getting it all done. We want to connect with God as we remember His love and relish the gift of His Son.

God, thank You for the gift of rest. Help me to accept the gift You've given me. Show me how I can incorporate restful times to draw nearer to You in my holiday routines. I want to discern the most important way to spend my time. Help me to value rest the way You do. I long to understand what it means to experience complete rest in You. In Jesus' name I pray, amen.

Questions for Reflection

Where is the Lord calling you to grow in the area of rest?

With that in mind, what can you do, or not do, to truly rest in that area?

What can you do this week to carve out a day or a few hours for restful soul nourishment?

A PRACTICAL APPROACH

Sit down and make your own list of ideas to try that would be completely restful for you. Some guiding questions might be:

- Do I feel farther from or closer to God after this activity?
- Does this rest produce anything besides nearness to the Lord?

Schedule a time this week to work your way down the list of restful activities. Find a lasting calm in your soul as you reflect on God's incredible gift to you—His Son.

⚬ Day 22 ⚬

PLANNING FOR REST

When the dew evaporated, a flaky substance as fine as frost blanketed the ground. The Israelites were puzzled when they saw it. "What is it?" they asked each other. They had no idea what it was.

And Moses told them, "It is the food the LORD has given you to eat. These are the LORD's instructions: Each household should gather as much as it needs. Pick up two quarts for each person in your tent."

So the people of Israel did as they were told. Some gathered a lot, some only a little. But when they measured it out, everyone had just enough. Those who gathered a lot had nothing left over, and those who gathered only a little had enough. Each family had just what it needed.

Then Moses told them, "Do not keep any of it until morning." But some of them didn't listen and kept some of it until morning. But by then it was full of maggots and had a terrible smell. Moses was very angry with them.

After this the people gathered the food morning by morning, each family according to its need. And as the sun became hot, the flakes they had not picked up melted and disappeared. On the sixth day, they gathered twice as much as usual—four quarts for each person instead of two. Then all the leaders of the community came and asked Moses for an explanation. He told them, "This is what the LORD commanded: Tomorrow will be a day of complete rest, a holy Sabbath day set apart for the LORD. So bake or boil as much as you want today, and set aside what is left for tomorrow."

So they put some aside until morning, just as Moses had commanded. And in the morning the leftover food was wholesome and good, without maggots or odor. Moses said, "Eat this food today, for today is a Sabbath day dedicated to the LORD. There will be no food on the ground today. You may gather the food for six days, but the seventh day is the Sabbath. There will be no food on the ground that day."

Some of the people went out anyway on the seventh day, but they found no food.
~ *Exodus 16:14-27*

I have to chuckle when I read the story of the Israelites in the wilderness. God provided manna from heaven. He gave them just enough for each day, but they wanted to try and gather a little extra just in case. The manna they tried to keep was rotten on the next day. I relate because I am so much like these hardheaded people. God promises to give us what we need for each day just like He provided manna for the people of Israel, but doubts and fears can easily creep into my mind as I wrestle to believe His promises in the midst of the difficulties of life. The Israelites had witnessed the Lord part the Red Sea and then use those same waters to drown their Egyptian enemies. Yet they still struggled with doubt.

We, too, have seen God at work in our midst. He provides for us and gives us His precious promises; and during Christmas we celebrate His ultimate gift—He sent His Son to die for our sins. Still, we "test" God sometimes by trying to do things our own way first. This is especially true when it comes to rest. We are no longer under the mandate of the Sabbath law. We don't have to adhere to the strict rules of observation of the Old Testament law. Christ came to set us free. Romans 6:14 says, "Sin is no longer your master, for you no longer live under the requirements of the law. Instead, you live under the freedom of God's grace."

While Sabbath is not a requirement, the concept behind it remains. God calls us to rest. In the days of Creation we find God resting on the seventh day. This wasn't because He was tired; He never sleeps (Psalm 121:4). Instead, He set this day of rest as a pattern for us. The Ten Commandments included Sabbath instructions.

We also find throughout the Law and the Prophets a call to take time for rest.

I can find myself like the Israelites in this passage skirting around the issue. I think things such as:

- I'll rest after Christmas.
- I don't have time to rest.
- If other people would help me, I might be able to rest.
- Maybe next year I'll have a more restful schedule.

Have you ever had thoughts like these? God calls us to make rest a priority. He wants us to stop and give our body, mind, and soul some time to be restored. He didn't create any of us to be the Energizer Bunny. Instead, He designed us to take time to rest regularly. The psalmist wrote, "We are merely moving shadows, / and all our busy rushing ends in nothing" (Psalm 39:6).

Yet some of us are running around like our hair is on fire. We need to buy the perfect gift for a long list of people. We have to attend every function we are invited to. We must respond to every comment people leave on our social media sites. At the end of it all, what have we accomplished? God has called us to do good works, but He has also called us to rest. This requires planning and great intentionality in our harried culture. In order to enjoy the rest He modeled for us, some preparation is required. Our preparation might include

- cooking double one day so we can rest the next day,
- blocking off some time in our schedules allocated only for rest,
- saying no to requests so that we can guard the time needed to rest, or
- working a little longer one day in order to rest the next.

Preparation may look different for you. A young mom may need to ask a friend to watch her children for a few hours so she can rest. Then she could watch that friend's kids another day in order for that mom to take some time to relax. High-stress jobs can demand hours of time. Preparing for rest might mean setting boundaries with time set aside to unplug from emails, calls, or texts. Others may be retired or have more margin in their schedules, but opportunities to volunteer or serve people can fill their calendars. It is not about how much time we have but more about how we spend that time. Each of us will have a unique situation when it comes to preparing for rest.

The time spent getting ready for rest will be well worth it as we experience a greater connection to God and restoration of our spirit.

Lord, help me to prepare for rest in the midst of the Christmas holiday. Show me where I can carve out some time to be still and listen to You. Give me the foresight to think ahead and discover how I can work in ways that allow for times of rest. In Jesus' name I pray, amen.

QUESTIONS FOR REFLECTION

When in the coming week could you set aside some time for rest (whether it's a day or a few hours)?

What preparations would you need to make in order to have some time for rest?

How do you think working harder one day so that you could rest more the next would affect your week?

A Practical Approach

As Christmas Day approaches, think through what would need to happen so that December 25th could actually be restful for you.

- Is there some food you could make ahead of time?
- Are there gifts that could be totally ready?
- What help could you enlist so that you could have at least a few hours to just enjoy the day?

Consider any Christmas preparations that aren't yet accomplished. Is there anything that you could give yourself permission to let go? Maybe this year you won't send cards. Perhaps you don't have to go to that one party. You could still do some baking, but you could make fewer varieties of cookies. What could you let go of in order to carve out some time for quiet and rest?

Day 23

REDEEMING THE MOMENTS

"Be still, and know that I am God!
I will be honored by every nation.
I will be honored throughout the world."
~ *Psalm 46:10*

This is what the Sovereign LORD,
the Holy One of Israel, says:
"Only in returning to me
and resting in me will you be saved.
In quietness and confidence is your strength.
But you would have none of it."
~ *Isaiah 30:15*

Some of my favorite moments of rest during the holidays do not include lengthy periods of time to unwind, because those just don't usually happen for me. However, there are little glimpses of quiet that I treasure. At night, when all the kids have been tucked into bed, I head down the hall toward the stairs. With a house full of teenagers it seems to be getting later and later that the house is quiet. At the end of a long day, I want to finish up loading a few dishes in the dishwasher and picking up things that have been left out before crawling into bed. However, with the glow of the lights from the tree beckoning me, I will often stop and sit on the couch. In the stillness and quiet I take just a few minutes to be still. These tranquil moments after a packed day are something precious that gives me space to

- think about God,
- get off my feet,
- allow my mind to take a break, and
- soak in the quiet.

My body and mind are too tired to accomplish any mental planning or physical work. It is a time just to think about God and revel in what He has done. He sent His one and only Son to earth. It still blows me away that the God who created everything loves me. He is holy and perfect, and yet He sacrificed Jesus in order to restore His relationship with me. It gives me pause. It overwhelms me. My Creator loves me, and He is crazy about you too.

I find that there are many spaces in my day where I could stop and be still. While I'm waiting at a red light or the checkout line at the grocery store, I have the opportunity to do something with my thoughts. Too often my phone has become all-consuming. Any time I have a free moment my hands have this pull to locate my phone and check my email, scroll through social media, or look something up on the internet. It has become second nature.

Instead of using the moments of white space in my day to pause, rest, and think about God, I yearn for a little more information. Whether it's an email with yet another promotional offer of something I should buy or the news update on how my sister's friend's cousin's dog is doing after surgery, I have become a notification junkie. I struggle to turn off the stream of information that is available at my fingertips and just sit quietly.

During a season when so much is rolling around in our brains, we can choose to redeem the small moments scattered throughout our day to be still. In the Book of Isaiah, God said our strength would come in quietness and confidence. The Hebrew word used in 30:15 for "quietness" is *shaqat*. It means, "to be quiet, be tranquil, be at peace, be quiet, rest, lie still, be undisturbed" (biblestudytools.com).

Undisturbed is a wonderful word. While people in our lives can cause interruptions, so often disturbances of our own making prevent us from the quietness referred to in Psalm 46:10 and Isaiah 30:15. I wonder if the quietness isn't just the absence of talking but a real stillness in the mind and body. Returning to thoughts of the Lord and resting in what He has done for us will be strength for us.

Large blocks of time to rest may not be realistic as the days of December draw toward Christmas. However, you can redeem some moments of quietness and trust in God throughout your day. Look for a few moments today during a lunch break, while waiting on others, or right before you head to bed. Take some time to quiet your thoughts and think about God. Rest in His great love for you.

God, help me to be still. Reveal the minutes I spend on frivolous things that I could be spending in quietness and confidence. I pray that You would give me Your strength to celebrate Christmas in a way that honors You. Help me to have eyes to see You throughout each day as I quiet my body and mind to know that You are God. In Jesus' name I pray, amen.

QUESTIONS FOR REFLECTION

Are there minutes in your day that you spend waiting?

What do you usually do while waiting or in the discretionary moments in your day?

How could you redeem those times to be still before God?

A PRACTICAL APPROACH

Today when you find yourself waiting for your computer to come on, the stoplight to turn green, or any other moments you discover, take some time to be quiet and rehearse God's attributes. Go through the alphabet and think of something about God for each letter. For example:

> A—God, you are Alpha and Omega.
> B—You are beautiful.
> C—Jesus, you are the Christ.

You get the idea. See how far you get through the alphabet, starting several different times throughout the day. Notice how your attitude and thoughts are affected by celebrating Jesus' birthday with quiet moments of worship peppered throughout your day.

Day 24

REST FOR THE SOUL

This is what the LORD says:
"Stop at the crossroads and look around.
    Ask for the old, godly way, and walk in it.
Travel its path, and you will find rest for your souls.
    But you reply, 'No, that's not the road we want!'"
~ Jeremiah 6:16

Over the years our family has dealt with quite a few health problems including asthma and alopecia, as well as minor colds and ear infections. So we have had some experience with prescriptions given by doctors. Some of them are taken every day and refilled monthly, and others are short-term courses for specific problems. The reason for each prescription might vary, but ultimately they are prescribed by a doctor as a way to help with a physical problem.

For the prescription to work as best as possible, two things have to happen:

- First, you have to get it filled.
- Second, you have to follow the instructions and take it as directed.

God used the prophet Jeremiah to deliver a prescription to His people. As the Great Physician, God wanted His people to have rest for the soul. However, in order to get to rest, some steps must be followed. We, too, can learn God's prescriptive path for rest. The holiday season is a time when we need rest more than any other. The increased activities and responsibilities can stress us out. So, here is what we must do:

Stop at the crossroads. This can be the hardest part of the prescription for rest. I can think of two reasons for a stop sign. The first is that we don't want to hit someone. If we don't stop in life, we might crash into someone else. We might expend a lot of time and energy working hard, but we can plow people over in the process if we don't stop and see how our tone, planning, and decisions affect others. I have found myself preparing for Christmas activities doing a lot of cooking and cleaning. My children have walked in the door from school, and I have given sharp orders telling them what jobs I need them to do. I don't always realize how I am treating them. I don't stop to consider what has happened in their day. They might need a snack and a moment to unwind after a long day of school. I can mow right over their needs to get my agenda accomplished. I need to stop and be careful not to crash into my children in my hurry and scurry.

The second reason for a stop sign is that it gives an opportunity for a change of direction. When we take the time to stop, we can decide whether to turn toward a new path. What crossroads are you currently facing? Are you in need of turning to the right or the left in hopes of finding a road that's a little less bumpy when it comes to your Christmas agenda?

After Jeremiah warned the people of Judah to stop at the crossroads, he told them to:

Look around. The apostle Paul gave the church at Ephesus similar instructions. He said, "See then that ye walk circumspectly, not as fools, but as wise" (Ephesians 5:15 KJV). Walking in a circle means trying to see the whole situation from different points of view. We need to be careful to walk circumspectly so that we can try to put ourselves in the shoes of others and evaluate what a situation looks like from another vantage point. This is especially true when it comes to our friends or extended family members in making holiday plans. Does everything have to be done to benefit us? Are there others who need to be considered above our desires? Jesus, the one whose birth we celebrate, said it this way, "Look beneath the surface so you can judge correctly" (John 7:24).

In order to have rest for your own soul, ask God help you to see things clearly. Once you have taken a good hard look at things—then move on to asking for God's wisdom.

Ask for the old, godly way. During the Christmas season, we can ask the Lord to help us see His way. How would He like us to celebrate? What posture would He want us to take? This means spending time in prayer seeking God's wisdom rather than our own. Where do you need wisdom right now? Ask God to help you see His way in it.

The last part of the prescription is to:

Travel the path. Many of us are educated beyond our obedience. We want to learn some new truth, but we struggle to obey the things we already know: Pray. Forgive. Love. Study the Word. Serve others.

As we approach our celebrations of Christ's birth, where is God calling you to travel the path of obedience to Him? What will bring rest for your soul? Taking the time to ask for the old, godly way and then doing the things we know God is calling us to do are necessary for the soul to rest and fully take effect.

This prescription does have some side effects:

- You'll stand out from the crowd when you experience peace and rest in your soul.
- Others might begin to ask you about the prescription so they can experience rest too.

I pray that we would take God's prescription through Jeremiah to heart so that rest can be not just physical but also spiritual this Christmas.

Lord, help me to find Your rest. Show me where I need to stop, look, ask, and obey. I desire rest for the soul. I am weary with all I need to accomplish in the coming days. Help me to stop and rest completely in You. Give me Your eyes to see clearly what is going on around me so that I can follow You wholeheartedly. Thank You for offering me this prescription for rest for the soul. In Jesus' name I pray, amen.

QUESTIONS FOR REFLECTION

Does the phrase "rest for the soul" describe you typically at Christmas?

Is stopping, asking, looking, or obeying the most difficult part of this prescription for you?

What is one way you can implement this prescription in your routine today?

A PRACTICAL APPROACH

Take the appropriate steps to identify a way to rest in the Lord:

- Identify one decision you must make today or in the next few days. It can be a small decision such as what type of gift to buy, which organization to donate money to before the end of the year, or which events not to attend this week. It might be a big decision such as whether to adopt a child, take a trip, or reestablish contact with an estranged relative. Remember that every decision is a spiritual one no matter how big or small it is. God delights in the details of our lives. He is the Lord of both the big and the small things.

- Write the decision that came to mind in a journal, on a piece of paper, or in the notes in your phone.

- Now when it comes to that decision, write what it would be like for you to:

  1. **Stop.** Think about how you can slow down from your regular schedule and really put some time and effort into seeking rest for the soul. Remember that rest for the body and rest for the soul may not be the same thing.

  2. **Look around.** Write down the different scenarios of choices you could make at this crossroads. How will others be affected? What would be the impact of this decision in one month, one year, ten years?

  3. **Ask.** Write out a prayer asking God to give you His wisdom as you consider your choices. Ask what the

old, godly way of faith would look like when applied
to your decision.

4. **Travel the path.** Now write what it would be like to
follow God's wisdom gained through stopping, looking, and asking.

Enjoy the rest for your soul in this area as God graciously grants
you His wisdom!

Day 25

ENTERING GOD'S REST

God's promise of entering his rest still stands, so we ought to tremble with fear that some of you might fail to experience it. For this good news—that God has prepared this rest—has been announced to us just as it was to them. But it did them no good because they didn't share the faith of those who listened to God. For only we who believe can enter his rest. As for the others, God said,

> *"In my anger I took an oath:*
> *'They will never enter my place of rest,'"*

even though this rest has been ready since he made the world. We know it is ready because of the place in the Scriptures where it mentions the seventh day: "On the seventh day God rested from all his work." But in the other passage God said, "They will never enter my place of rest."

So God's rest is there for people to enter, but those who first heard this good news failed to enter because they disobeyed God. So God set another time for entering his rest, and that time is today. God announced this through David much later in the words already quoted:

> *"Today when you hear his voice,*
> *don't harden your hearts."*

Now if Joshua had succeeded in giving them this rest, God would not have spoken about another day of rest still to come. So there is a special rest still waiting for the people of God. For all who have entered into God's rest have rested from their labors, just as God did after creating the world. So let us do our best to enter that rest. But if we disobey God, as the people of Israel did, we will fall.
~ Hebrews 4:1-11

Christmas is usually a restful day for me. Our children tend to sleep a little later and wake to search for their stockings. We eat cinnamon rolls, open gifts, and then often play games together or spend time assembling new items. Since both our families live far away, we don't have to rush off to anyone's house or attend large gatherings. It is usually just our immediate family relaxing and spending time together.

The writer of Hebrews talked much about rest, but it isn't just the kind we experience on Christmas Day. He wasn't referring to a relaxed schedule or inactivity. Hebrews 4:1-11 refers to the ultimate rest we find in Christ. Celebrating Christ's birth reminds us that He came to die. He died to atone for our sin so we could experience rest in our relationship with God.

God's offer of rest still stands for us. The good news of the gospel is that we can enter it. Today's Scripture passage makes it clear that His rest is for those who believe. That is how we can enter ultimate rest. We must accept God's word by faith. That is what will bring us rest.

Sin brought chaos and separation to the harmony that Creation had with God. When Adam and Eve sinned they were banished from the garden. They no longer enjoyed fellowship with God in the same way. Yet from the very beginning God had a plan to restore rest between a holy God and sinful humans. In Genesis 3:15 we find the first mention of Messiah.

> "And I will cause hostility between you and the woman,
>   and between your offspring and her offspring.
> He will strike your head,
>   and you will strike his heel."

God sent His Son to deliver us from sin and death. Through faith in Him we can enter God's promise of rest. Have you entered God's rest through faith? Even if life doesn't feel very restful because of difficult circumstances, physical illness, or relational strain, we can have rest in our relationship with God through faith in Christ.

Scripture tell us that today is the day to enter God's rest. The writer of Hebrews instructs us not to harden our hearts. So we need a soft heart with obedience coupled with faith in order to enter into a restful state of peace with God. If you have accepted God's invitation to follow Christ, you have a restored relationship with God.

He has justified you through the blood of Christ. This means the Father sees you "just as if you have never sinned." You have rest from the penalty of sin. God is in the process of sanctifying you. Every day He conforms you more to the image of His Son as you grow in faith and obedience. You are being saved from the power of sin in your life on a daily basis. One day, we will be glorified. This means we will have ultimate rest as we are removed from the very presence of sin.

We don't have to work to earn God's favor. He offers it to us as a gift. When we accept His grace through the blood of Christ, we have entered God's rest positionally; we are also in the process of entering it practically on a daily basis, and one day we will fully enjoy God's rest from sin and death.

Lord, thank You for offering me Your rest. Help me to enter into Your rest today. Show me the way of faith and obedience. Thank You for sending Your one and only Son to earth so that I can have peace with You. Today is the day I want to soften my heart before You so that I may know Your rest more fully. In Jesus' name I pray, amen.

QUESTIONS FOR REFLECTION

How does God's salvation through Christ bring rest into your life practically?

What are some practical ways you can be intentional to enter God's rest?

How can you experience God's salvation rest even when life is tumultuous?

A Practical Approach

Spend some time today thinking about God's salvation in your life. Reflect on the meaning of Christmas and its implications of rest for you. If you aren't sure that you have ever made the decision to enter God's rest by accepting His gospel message, today is the day! Embrace the gospel message:

- **God is love.** "For this is how God loved the world: He gave his one and only Son, so that everyone who believes in him will not perish but have eternal life." (John 3:16)
- **Humans have sinned.** "For everyone has sinned; we all fall short of God's glorious standard." (Romans 3:23)
- **Christ paid the penalty.** "But God showed his great love for us by sending Christ to die for us while we were still sinners." (Romans 5:8)
- **We need to receive Christ.** "But to all who believed him and accepted him, he gave the right to become children of God." (John 1:12)

If you have made this decision, reflect on how these truths are not just a past experience but a present reality in your life.

Day 26

RESTING VERSUS ESCAPING

And now, dear brothers and sisters, one final thing. Fix your thoughts on what is true, and honorable, and right, and pure, and lovely, and admirable. Think about things that are excellent and worthy of praise.
~ Philippians 4:8

I was talking about rest with a Jewish believer in Christ who mentioned that he observed a Friday evening to Saturday evening Sabbath rest each week. He told me that rest should draw us nearer to God, so he set this time aside for that purpose.

My life would radically change if I set aside twenty-four hours each week to rest and connect with Jesus. I reflected on some of the ways I tend to unwind after the hustle and bustle of the holidays or even just at the end of a long week. Rather than engaging in restful activities to draw me close to the Lord, I often turn to modes of escape. It can be easy to give ourselves permission to indulge our flesh after the intensity of holiday preparation and celebration. After all, we baked all those cookies, wrapped all those presents, attended all those gatherings, and put up all those decorations. Don't we deserve a break? God desires that we get some needed rest, but too many times I'm drawn to things that don't leave me feeling restored and closer to the Lord. At the end of a *Law and Order* marathon and several bowls of ice cream, I don't typically experience a healthier mind and body.

So in the aftermath of the holidays, we must ask ourselves this question: What restful activities will bring us closer to God and be restorative to our souls? The answer to this question for me includes things such as:

- **Sleep.** When I am deprived of bodily rest, I get cranky and short-tempered. I open myself up to temptation when I am tired. Sleeping makes me feel closer to God and more pleasant in general.
- **Walking.** Taking a walk in a park or nature preserve brings me closer to the Lord as I breathe in fresh air and observe God's creation. It can be tough to do this depending on the weather, but even ten minutes outside can do wonders for the spirit.
- **Reading.** Whether it's Scripture, a good novel, or a marriage, parenting, or self-help book, reading is relaxing for me.
- **Writing.** Not everyone enjoys pouring his or her heart out on paper, but journaling is a way that I can reflect on my feelings and concerns and helps me process what God is teaching me.

Your list might be totally different. Organizing a closet, gathering with people, or playing a game might help you rest. Taking time for reflective activities will be a key for us to learn to rest in a way that connects us with God rather than providing a temporary escape. We can use Philippians 4:8 as a good test for our leisure activities. We can ask if this restful endeavor helps us to focus on things that are:

- true
- honorable
- right
- pure

- lovely
- admirable
- excellent
- worthy of praise

When we find things that fit these criteria, we usually walk away feeling restored and rested. Media and junk food might make us feel good initially, but they will not ultimately leave us with the connection with God that we desire. While we may not be able to devote a full twenty-four hours to resting every week, we can carve out restorative time on a regular basis.

Lord, help me to learn to rest rather than escape after stressful activities. I want to surrender even my leisure time to You. Guide me to engage in restful activities that help me grow closer to You. In Jesus' name I pray, amen.

QUESTIONS FOR REFLECTION

What types of activities help you feel closer to God?

What is restful to both your body and mind?

How can Philippians 4:8 help you discover more restful leisure choices?

A Practical Approach

Make a list of all the things you do to unwind. Then run them through the Philippians 4:8 passage. Ask a few friends what types of things help them feel closer to God and are restful for the body, mind, and soul. Try out something new today to rest and draw near to the Lord.

Day 27

BALANCE

Therefore, since we are surrounded by such a huge crowd of witnesses to the life of faith, let us strip off every weight that slows us down, especially the sin that so easily trips us up. And let us run with endurance the race God has set before us. We do this by keeping our eyes on Jesus, the champion who initiates and perfects our faith.
~ Hebrews 12:1-2a

I don't mean to say that I have already achieved these things or that I have already reached perfection. But I press on to possess that perfection for which Christ Jesus first possessed me. No, dear brothers and sisters, I have not achieved it, but I focus on this one thing: Forgetting the past and looking forward to what lies ahead, I press on to reach the end of the race and receive the heavenly prize for which God, through Christ Jesus, is calling us.
~ Philippians 3:12-14

Look straight ahead,
     and fix your eyes on what lies before you.
~ Proverbs 4:25

Most of the time I feel as if I'm trying to juggle five balls in the air and two always seem to fall to the ground. If my house is clean, my emails are answered, and I've packed my kids' lunches, I feel pretty good about what I've accomplished. Then I realize that I've neglected to put away the holiday decorations or pay all the bills. It can be challenging to keep all those balls in the air at the same time. Especially as we look forward to a new year, we desire to find balance. Maybe this year we will do better when it comes to juggling marriage, home management, parenting, work, and church and volunteer commitments.

Will there ever be a day when we become expert jugglers? Or should we learn to celebrate the balls we are keeping in the air instead of living in guilt over the dropped balls?

Finding the right balance reminds me of a picture of an elephant standing on a beach ball. Balance for me seems about that likely. Physical balance isn't one of my strong suits. At my aerobics classes, I would literally fall over sometimes when we stretched. Then my instructor gave me some advice that really helped. She told me to find something to focus on—a spot on the floor or an object on the wall. When I fixed my eyes in one place, I was able to maintain my balance much better.

I find the same is true when it comes to balancing the demands of life. When I fix my eyes in one place—on the Lord Jesus Christ, it changes everything. As I attempt to balance all the demands of daily life, all too often my focus rests on the things I haven't done. I compare myself to others who seem to always be on time, their kids' socks match (mine sometimes wore mittens on their feet when I was behind on the laundry), and the food they bring to the classroom parties looks like it required hours of Pinterest surfing. When my focus is on my failures or comparing, I often lose my sense of balance and feel like I'm failing. When I don't put my focus on Jesus, I often just hit the ground running from the time my feet hit the floor. I find myself tackling whatever task seems right in front of me at the moment. Whatever I'm doing at the time, I have this looming sense that I should be doing something else. It is not very restful at all. Instead I need to combat my negative self-talk with truth that brings calm in the midst of the mundane:

- "Your emails can wait; your family needs clean clothes. Enjoy the simplicity of the task."
- "People and the Word of God are the only two eternal things; this house will not last forever, the souls of my kids will. Be okay with dishes in the sink."
- "Even though it feels like you are letting others down in this moment, saying no to them means saying yes to your kids."

I find peace comes even with several dropped balls on the ground when I keep my eyes fixed on Jesus in the midst of the juggling act. I can celebrate the accomplishment of the things that I am getting done, even if it's a game of Chutes and Ladders with a four-year-old.

As you seek balance in your life, remember to fix your eyes in one place when you feel like you're about to fall. Jesus will help you stand and also pick you up when you fall. We may never find perfect balance, but we can enjoy life much better with the confidence that comes with a focus on Christ and the leading of the Holy Spirit.

God, help me to focus on You. I want to rest in what You have called me to do, not the balls I feel like I am always dropping. Help me to see where You are at work in the details of my day. Thank You for all You have given me to do. Show me how I can do it for Your glory and bask in the peace that You bring along with it. In Jesus' name I pray, amen.

QUESTIONS FOR REFLECTION

Where does negative self-talk seek to steal your peace?

How does focusing on God help you from self-shaming?

Where is God calling you to rest in what He is doing in your life instead of always wanting to do and be more?

A PRACTICAL APPROACH

Make a list of everything you feel guilty about right now. Now go back through each item and check the ones that you actually have some measure of control over. Ask the Lord to show you any action steps He might want you to take. Also, prayerfully consider what balls are OK to leave on the floor. We can't do everything and be everything to everyone. Instead, we must strive for balance.

Day 28

NEW STRENGTH

"Have you never heard?
Have you never understood?
The LORD is the everlasting God,
the Creator of all the earth.
He never grows weak or weary.
No one can measure the depths of his understanding.
He gives power to the weak
and strength to the powerless.
Even youths will become weak and tired,
and young men will fall in exhaustion.
But those who trust in the LORD will find new strength.
They will soar high on wings like eagles.
They will run and not grow weary.
They will walk and not faint."
~ Isaiah 40:28-31

As one year comes to an end and another begins, it can be a time to consider some things we might like to change. Some people roll their eyes at the thought of New Year's resolutions or written goals, but I find them helpful. If we aim for nothing, we hit it every time.

So taking time each year to evaluate different areas of our lives and asking God for wisdom when it comes to things we would like to see happen can be a good practice. Short-term goals, dreams, and action steps to accomplish the things we believe God might have in our future can be a good thing. God says we can find new strength when we trust in Him. How can we walk in this strength He promises us? I want to run and not grow weary. The problem is that I run and run and run without allowing Him to restore me. In order to soar on wings like eagles, I must be intentional in my pursuit of God.

One of the first times I filled out a goal sheet for a new year I didn't want to do it. I was one of those eye-rollers. I like to fly by the seat of my pants rather than write out goals in order to soar on eagles' wings. Unfortunately that doesn't always work out so well. At the time I was being coached by an older woman through monthly phone conversations to help me grow as a Christian. I wrote out my thoughts on the form she gave me for setting goals and noticed the category of "Dreams." I daringly jotted down that someday I wanted to write a book.

She noticed those scant words and began asking questions. She asked what a first step down that path would look like. Every month I had to review this goal sheet and give updates. I realized that I needed someone to push me to follow through on the things I felt the Lord was calling me to do.

When it comes to rest, I know I'm not going to stumble upon it. I must take the time to evaluate where I have discretionary time and how I can implement rest into my regular schedule. At the end of December, I have my family sit down with me in this process and work on their own goals. As they moan and groan at yet another activity forced on them by their mother, I put a page with a graph similar to this in front of them:

	Short-Range Goals	How I Plan to Accomplish My Short-Range Goals	Dreams	How I Plan to Accomplish My Dreams
Personal Family				
Spiritual Moral				
Caring Giving				
Health Fitness				

I tell them that they don't have to fill out every space. They can choose only two areas in which to set goals. After their complaining subsides, they actually get quiet and begin to write things in the boxes. I put their papers in a folder and take them out at the beginning of each month so we can review our progress.

Under the health and fitness section, I set some goals for rest this year. It is an important personal goal. Every biblical celebration in Scripture includes rest. God made it a priority for His people from the Creation days to the Mosaic law. The New Testament sets us free from the law but doesn't negate the concept of rest. I want to learn to draw nearer to God by slowing down and connecting with Him on a regular basis. I know rest won't happen in my life accidentally. We can't continue to do the same things and expect different results. Just as I have to be intentional in exercise, writing, prayer, and studying God's Word, rest will need to be a discipline I pursue.

How about you? In the next year would you like to rest more? Is there another area of life where God is calling you to set a goal and have some accountability to meet it? As we trust Him more, we find our weariness subsiding. He allows us to soar as we pursue Jesus with our whole heart.

Lord, help me to aim for rest in the coming year. Show me a few small changes I can make to live out the desires of my heart. I want to know You more. Help me to establish spiritual rhythms that will draw me closer to You. Help me to find others to walk alongside me who will encourage me in my pursuit of You. In Jesus' name I pray, amen.

QUESTIONS FOR REFLECTION

What is one spiritual goal you could set for the coming year?

How have you grown weak or weary lately?

What big dreams come to mind as you think about your future?

A PRACTICAL APPROACH

Set aside an hour in the coming week to fill out the goal graph in this chapter. Especially consider any goals you would like to incorporate regarding rest in the coming year.

Day 29

YIELDING

Then Jesus said, "Come to me, all of you who are weary and carry heavy burdens, and I will give you rest. Take my yoke upon you. Let me teach you, because I am humble and gentle at heart, and you will find rest for your souls."
~ Matthew 11:28-29

These verses from Matthew 11 are some of my favorite in all of Scripture. Jesus offers us rest for our souls. All He asks of us is to take His yoke. He invites us to stop striving and rest in Him. This means following His way over ours. Since He is humble and gentle, we can trust that His instructions are better than whatever our inclinations might be.

I'm always trying to convince my kids to obey. If they will just listen the first time, do what I say, and follow our family rules, life will go much better for them (and me). We will extend them freedoms, build trust with them, and enjoy our time together so much more. Some of my kids "get this" more than others.

After all, the rules and standards we have set come out of our great love for our children. We want them to treat each other with respect, take care of their things, and learn to work hard because we know these practices will bring blessing and favor in their lives. Yet they constantly seem to resist by speaking harshly, leaving their socks all over the house, and asking to watch movies or wear clothing that they know we won't approve. They call our standards unfair and have even claimed on occasion that we are "ruining their lives."

When these situations come up (as they often do with four preteen/teens in the house), we stand our ground knowing that our heart for them is blessing not frustration. Throughout Scripture, I see God's parenting heart for us. He longs to shower us with favor, take care of us, and see us win the battles we our fighting. He calls us to lean hard into Him—His Spirit, His way, and His gentleness. Then we will find rest even in the midst of the many struggles we experience in life. God spells out very clearly His expectations and regulations for His people.

In Leviticus 26:1-13, God tells the Israelites that if they will "follow my decrees and are careful to obey my commands" (v. 3):

- He will send seasonal rains.
- The land will yield crops.
- The trees will produce fruit.
- "You will eat your fill and live securely in the land."
- He "will give you peace in the land, and you will be able to sleep with no cause for fear."
- He will protect you from enemies and wild animals.
- All your enemies will fall beneath the blows of your weapons.
- He will look favorably on you and multiply you.
- He will give a surplus of crops so that you will need to throw away leftovers to make room for more.
- He "will live among you, . . . walk among you, . . . be your God."
- You will "no longer be slaves. . . . you can walk with your heads held high."

This is how God wants us to live. As a parent, He wants to provide for us, protect us from danger, have victory over enemies, and have extras to share with others. He wants us to live without fear and "walk with our heads held high" (v. 13).

He goes on in the chapter to warn His people what disobedience brings. He says when they follow their own path, other nations would rule over them. They would "run even when no one is chasing you!" (v. 17). This passage mentions living in imagined fears three times. Another repeated regulation throughout Leviticus is rest. They were to rest on the Sabbath and let the land rest every seven years. God said if the Israelites disobey His rest rules, He would force the land to rest by taking them into exile.

Of course God's compassion even in His punishments win out. God says even when we disobey, He will walk with us through our consequences and restore us when we turn back to Him (vv. 44-45). In the way a parent can never forget her children, God never abandons us. He allows us to eat the bitter fruit of living our own way, but He longs to see us restored to the blessings of obedience when we turn to Him.

I pray your day is filled with obedience blessings as you love God and love people. Even when His commands seem frustrating or difficult, let's remember God is our perfect parent wanting to pour out His gifts on us through our obedience to Him.

Lord, I want to yield to You. Help me to lay down my heavy load and take Your yoke upon me. Thank You that Your burden is easy and light. I want to walk in your humility and gentleness today. If there is an area of disobedience in my life right now, I ask You to bring it to light. Show me how I can fully rest in You. In Jesus' name I pray, amen.

Questions for Reflection

What heavy burdens are weighing you down today?

How is God calling you to yield to Him?

What blessings have come into your life as a result of obedience?

A Practical Approach

Consider any areas of your life where you might be missing out on an obedience blessing. For example:

- Think about taking a fast from an area of temptation in your life for a set period of time (day, week, month). For example, if you struggle with eating too many sweet treats, try a week without dessert.
- Think about fasting from soul junk food, such as television or social media.
- Think about whether God is calling you to a greater obedience when it comes to gossip, self-care, or rest.

THE DAY OF SMALL BEGINNINGS

Then he said to me, "This is what the LORD says to Zerubbabel: It is not by force nor by strength, but by my Spirit, says the LORD of Heaven's Armies. Nothing, not even a mighty mountain, will stand in Zerubbabel's way; it will become a level plain before him! And when Zerubbabel sets the final stone of the Temple in place, the people will shout: 'May God bless it! May God bless it!'

Then another message came to me from the LORD: "Zerubbabel is the one who laid the foundation of this Temple, and he will complete it. Then you will know that the LORD of Heaven's Armies has sent me. Do not despise these small beginnings, for the LORD rejoices to see the work begin, to see the plumb line in Zerubbabel's hand."

(The seven lamps represent the eyes of the LORD that search all around the world.)

~ Zechariah 4:6-10

We will need a little context for today's Scripture verses. The prophet Zechariah wrote during the time when the Jewish people were returning after seventy years in exile. He spoke about Zerubbabel, who led tens of thousands of Israelites out of Babylon and back to their own land. This was the same Promised Land of Canaan where Abraham lived; where Solomon built the temple; and that Babylon later conquered and destroyed. During the return from captivity there was much rebuilding to do because of the amount of rubble.

I love the story of the return found in the books of Ezra and

Nehemiah and also referred to by the prophets Haggai, Zechariah, and Malachi. The story of rebuilding is the narrative of all our lives. Whether we need to incorporate more godly rituals, do the hard work of strengthening relationships, or change the pattern of our lives to include rest, all of us have work to do. God says we can't do it with our own strength. He said through the prophet Zechariah that His Spirit would help us. He is the Lord of Heaven's Armies and that nothing can stand in our way when we invite His power into our rebuilding projects in life.

Sometimes I forget these principles from God's Word. I can fall into two extremes when it comes to any kind of makeover in my life. The first danger is to pull up my bootstraps and think I can conquer a life makeover project myself. If I need more rest, I will construct a detailed plan and force my way. The trouble is the weakness of my flesh. I get discouraged and quit. I talk myself into compromising my new strategies when they get hard. Has anyone else ever done this when starting a healthy eating plan? Whenever we begin to make changes, we will need the Lord's help if we are going to sustain the new behaviors over the long haul. There are no eight-, ten-, or twelve-step programs that will help us get the work done without God's Spirit giving us the power to truly change from the heart.

The second issue I have in rebuilding with better decisions is the discouragement I feel from the outset. I've tried to change before; it never sticks. How many times have I tried to rest more? I can start to believe it isn't in the cards for me. Yet the Lord tells us not to be discouraged. We will come up against difficulty. However, He says not even a mountain will stand in our way with the Lord of Heaven's Armies on our side. Mountains are high, strong, thick and seemingly immovable. This is the same illustration Jesus used when talking about faith. In Matthew 21:21, we read, "Then Jesus told them, 'I tell you the truth, if you have faith and don't doubt, you can do things like this and much more. You can even say to this mountain, "May you be lifted up and thrown into the sea," and it will happen.' "

So we must be careful in our personal *Total Christmas Makeover* to remember that we can't do the work on our own. However, we can believe in faith, lean into God's Spirit, and begin rebuilding a closer connection with our beautiful Savior. He is cheering us on. In fact, He tells us not to despise the day of small beginnings. He delights to see the work begin.

We can continue to bring the ashes of our lives to our gracious God and watch Him transform the rubble into beauty. Our part is the coming. In humility and surrender we admit our need for God's help. Then He enables us by His Spirit and takes joy in doing the transforming work in our lives.

Lord, thank You for Your Spirit. Help me not to strive in my own strength to make my holiday full of rituals, relationships, and rest. Instead, I ask You to guide and help me to see where changes are needed. Thank You for delighting in the work beginning in my heart and mind. Lord, I believe in faith that You will complete the work You are starting in me.

QUESTIONS FOR REFLECTION

Is there one specific area where God is calling you to make some changes in your patterns, attitudes, or behaviors?

How have you been relying on your own might or strength to change? How has that been working for you?

What are some ways you have seen your faith grow in the past? What might God be challenging you to do today in order to grow more in mountain-moving faith?

A PRACTICAL APPROACH

Reflect on other days of small beginnings in your life. Consider times when

- you started a new job;
- you began a new class or educational pursuit;
- you were at the beginning of a new relationship that has grown and matured since; or
- you began a spiritual discipline such as prayer, Bible study, or attending church.

Thank the Lord for the days of small beginnings in your past. Now take some time to ask Him what He might be calling you to build or rebuild in your life in the coming year. Is there a new spiritual rhythm, relationship, ministry, or attitude He is calling you toward?

Identify one word for the coming year that sums up what you hear from the Lord. Write it in the front of your Bible, journal, or in the margin of today's devotion, and remember this as the day of small beginnings. Soak in God's delight over this word as you pursue Him more deeply in the coming year.

Day 31

THE REST OF THE STORY

When we were utterly helpless, Christ came at just the right time and died for us sinners. Now, most people would not be willing to die for an upright person, though someone might perhaps be willing to die for a person who is especially good. But God showed his great love for us by sending Christ to die for us while we were still sinners. And since we have been made right in God's sight by the blood of Christ, he will certainly save us from God's condemnation. For since our friendship with God was restored by the death of his Son while we were still his enemies, we will certainly be saved through the life of his Son. So now we can rejoice in our wonderful new relationship with God because our Lord Jesus Christ has made us friends of God.
~ *Romans 5:6-11*

As we pack away our Christmas decorations and get ready to fall back into our usual routines, let's not lose the wonder of what we just celebrated. Through our rituals, relationships, and rest, I hope we remembered and relished what God has done for us.

He sent His one and only Son to step out of eternity and into time—at just the right time. He did this out of His great love for us. Christ came as a baby but died as a suffering servant. These verses in Romans tell us that the death of Jesus restored our friendship with God.

So we can enter this year as friends of God. The rest of the story will be written as we walk in fellowship with God because of the blood of His Son. Seasons of celebration are wonderful. We get the opportunity to

- attend special church services,
- gather with family and friends,
- express generosity toward others with gifts, and
- remember all that the Lord has done for us.

As we head back into the regular routines of life, let's continue to walk in friendship with God. We can choose some spiritual rhythms that will help us stay connected to our Creator throughout the coming weeks and months.

Friends talk with each other. They spend time together. If we want to know God better in the coming year, we will want to carve out regular patterns of prayer and studying His Word. What will that look like for you? Will it mean getting up a little earlier each day or staying up a little later?

Perhaps joining a Bible study, Sunday School class, or small group through your church might help you deepen your friendship with God. Take some time as we close our devotional time together to ask God how you can grow in your relationship with Him in the coming year.

Wouldn't it be amazing if at this time next year, you could say that you dove more deeply into the life and teaching of Jesus? What if we were so immersed in the promises of God that they dominated our thoughts and spilled out on others in the midst of the challenges of coming year? What if we kept the spirit of Christmas all year long as we remembered the gift of Christ in our lives?

It won't look the same for every person, but we all can grow in faith through continued participation in spiritual rituals, relationships, and rest. God did some amazing things this past year, but I believe the best is yet to be. He has new adventures for you in the coming year, such as

- people for you to serve,
- Scripture for you to study,
- goals for your to accomplish, and
- rest for you to enjoy.

He doesn't force your hand, but He offers you His friendship through His Son, Jesus. Let's embrace the wonder of His gospel today and everyday as we worship the God who saw our helplessness and made a way for us to draw near to Him.

Father, we don't want to lose the wonder of what You have done by sending Christ to earth. Thank You for seeing our need and making a way for us to find our way back to You. Help us not to take lightly Your offer of friendship. Lord, may this be the year that we know You more and enter into Your rest in close fellowship with You. In Jesus' name I pray, amen.

QUESTIONS FOR REFLECTION

Where is God calling you to make changes in your spiritual rhythms?

Is there something He is calling you to add to your spiritual rituals?

Is there something He is calling you to let go of in order to rest in Him?

A Practical Approach

Friends often give each other special gifts, and God has given you His Son. Find a physical object you will see every day to remind you that God offers you His friendship through Christ. Whether it's a new picture for your wall, a single Christmas decoration you will leave out, or a special piece of art or jewelry, give yourself a physical item to help you remember God's gifts of ritual, relationships, and rest throughout the year.